THE STARTUP PITCH

Published by **SpeakValue, Ltd.**
Palo Alto, Ca.

For more information, contact
support@speakvalue.com

Version 2.0
ISBN 978-0-9911137-0-5

www.pitchpower.org

Conceptual & Editorial Design by
Sonia Oster

The Startup Pitch

A proven formula to win funding

To my parents Mandy and Bob
for teaching me the two real skills of life: love and independence.

Foreword

As an entrepreneur you will be asked to do many things, but none as hair-raising as that moment you are asked to deliver a pitch. That's when "the rubber meets the road" and you must share your idea with others who can help you succeed. Those few minutes are crucial.

Chris Lipp is an entrepreneur with a proven framework for pitching and a passion for helping fellow entrepreneurs tell their story. He has given all of us a gift by investing thousands of hours creating this primer for pitching which you are now holding in your hands (or reading on your kindle). He transparently shares his own failures and successes as an entrepreneur in the trenches trying to communicate to potential investors. But more than that, he has coached hundreds of fellow entrepreneurs, and interviewed and researched still more. In short, Chris Lipp has invested his time to understand pitching so all of us can benefit.

I urge you to buy The Startup Pitch, read it, and use it. This book (much like the method Chris will detail for you) meets a unique need in the marketplace. He's recognized that while other authors provide laundry lists of what to include, none shares a memorable, codified approach to guide the pitch itself. His approach is for you to embrace and use as you further your start-up pitching to potential investors.

Chris' approach is rapid fire, exactly what I find my students expect. Today's entrepreneurs are used to moving fast and adjusting on the go. In fact I have already sketched out his model for pitching numerous times with my own students to illustrate the key goals of a pitch. So I suggest you devour the book in short order, flagging items you want to revisit. Grasp the simplicity of Chris' 4-Point Formula and how your idea can be served by communicating in this way. Then, return to the book at a more leisurely pace as you build or refine your pitch. My prediction for this book is that dog-eared copies will make the rounds of incubators, shared work spaces, and dorm rooms as aspiring entrepreneurs begin to see the value in what Chris has created.

The Startup Pitch, written by an entrepreneur for entrepreneurs, directly reflects the task you face preparing a pitch. As I've read his drafts through the past year, I've seen the model emerge with greater clarity, much like the old Polaroid photographs that slowly appeared before your eyes (yeah, I'm dating myself now as a baby boomer.) Now Chris is ready to share it with all of you. The real gift is not the book, but what you do with it.

JD Schramm, Ed.D.
Founder,
Mastery in Communication Initiative
Stanford Graduate School of Business

Funding
6
Formula
2
5
Slides
Elements
3
1
4
Delivery
Investor

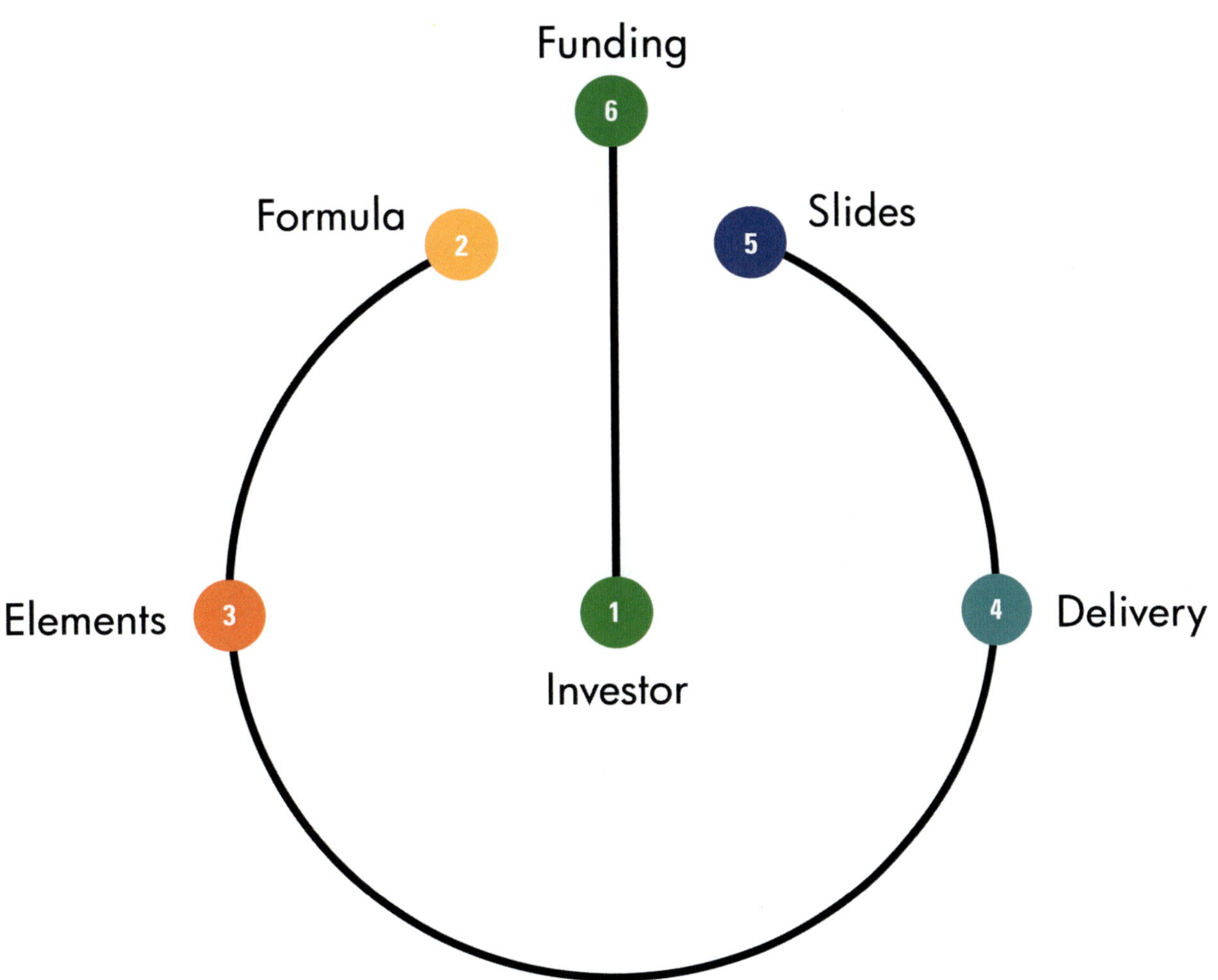

CONTENT

CHAPTER 1

REAL RULES

There is a formula for how to pitch successfully. You don't need to be a master presenter or persuader to win funding, it simply takes the right techniques applied consciously to capture capital.

1. REAL RULES

Beginning the quest
Audience focus
Clarity
You
Moving forward

Chapter 1 Real Rules

When CEO Howard Schultz hit the road to pitch Starbucks, he was rejected by over 200 investors. Schultz was a master marketer with strong people skills, but investors found reasons to reject. Perhaps they weren't convinced there was a market for gourmet coffee; maybe they were dubious of Schultz's business plan. Whatever the case, Schultz had to use every ounce of his talent to win enough investment and move the company into international stardom.

Most of us lack the talent of Howard Schultz, yet we still believe that after enough rejection there will be a light at the end of the tunnel for us too. However, the truth is that a typical VC may hear 750 pitches a year and invest in only three companies. That's less than one-half of 1 percent! To give some perspective, you have a much better chance of entering Harvard Business School and graduating into a large salary than you have of getting funding.

Why are so few companies funded? The primary reason is that VCs have limits on the time and money they can invest in startups. As a result, when you stand in front of investors, you're not just pitching your startup; you're competing against hundreds if not thousands of other startups for one of those few coveted spots.

So what does it take to win? The product certainly doesn't always speak for itself. Starbucks was rejected over 200 times! Nor do most entrepreneurs fail to prepare. Many of them, like you, read pitch advice online, practiced at startup events, and incorporated feedback from investors. However, these companies still failed to rise above the pack and attract investment. They are the amazing companies you will never know. Consider what happens to you if you don't win funding.

According to Paul Graham, founder of the famous incubator Y Combinator, "Raising money is the second hardest part of starting a startup. The hardest part is making something people want.... But the second biggest cause of death is probably the difficulty of raising money. Fundraising is brutal."

"RAISING MONEY IS THE SECOND HARDEST PART OF STARTING A STARTUP."

PAUL GRAHAM

Beginning the Quest

Silicon Valley is the startup capital of the world. Here, it's a circus of performances with startup energy bouncing off coffee shops, street corners, and corporate-sponsored seminars. There's a plethora of pitch opportunities. Casual events, accelerators, and large conferences give entrepreneurs the chance to pitch multiple times a week. These events generate connections that move entrepreneurs into VC rooms and on to business.

In 2011, I joined a startup and jumped into the Silicon Valley fray. We demoed our product at small events as well as large conferences like Founder Showcase and TechCrunch Disrupt. These large semi-annual conferences allowed us to set up a booth and practice our pitch to conference attendees. Some really lucky companies even won a spot on the main stage to pitch their startup to entire conference crowds.

As a communications coach at the Stanford Graduate School of Business, I was confident when I pitched our product at conferences. I was also a competitive public speaker and had bested thousands of contestants to win speech contests, giving me great delivery skills. Even so, when my company received the first opportunity to meet one-on-one with investors, I made sure to take time and research how to pitch effectively and win funding.

I went online and read advice from various bloggers. I perused books claiming I could learn to pitch like a pro. I modeled my slide deck off what I'd seen on Slideshare, including the infamous Mint.com slides. I even practiced informally at local events. When I walked into our first investor meeting, I was prepared.

We entered the meeting room, shook hands with the investors and sat down. I immediately started talking about our product. Just as quickly one of the investors lost interest and turned to stare out the window. I kept going when another investor stood up, walked around the table to my laptop and said "show me your web app." I tried to speak as I pulled up the website, but the investor was no longer listening. My words lost focus. Suddenly the only thing clear to me within those first few minutes of pitching was that we had failed.

That wasn't our first failure. I pitched and failed again, and again. Even though we ended up winning awards such as best-voted startup at conference events, I still failed to attract investment when it mattered.

I failed to attract investment because I had no definitive method on how to pitch a startup successfully. Pitch advice today focuses too much on presentation skills (which didn't help me!) and not enough on structure. Resources are scattered and often contradictory. So-called negotiation tactics written in pitch books are too difficult to implement.

Rejections are tough. Very, very tough. Startups are rarely casual activities – they're choices that reflect our careers and dreams. Every time an investor turned me away, I felt deep self-doubt and a sense of personal failure. We entrepreneurs know that rejection is a part of the experience, but it's not a fun part.

I left the startup after two years, but I never let go of my interest in pitching. I began to quest for a definitive pitch method. I interviewed the best communicators in the country, listened to top VCs, and analyzed dozens of pitches by companies that won funding. Leveraging my knowledge in presentations and marketing, I finally came up with the answer.

THERE IS A FORMULA FOR HOW TO PITCH SUCCESSFULLY

and I have outlined the formula in this book. The formula applies to investor meeting rooms as well as onstage at startup conferences. These techniques were used by Exactuals to close an oversubscribed seed round; they were implemented by GetAround, which now has over $19 million in funding; and they led Enigma to win the coveted $50,000 grand prize for best conference pitch at TechCrunch Disrupt. The goal of this formula is to win you funding.

As you move through the chapters, you will learn the 4-Point Formula required for every pitch and how to adjust the formula for different audiences. You will gain the techniques to pitch persuasively based on research in corporate communications. Towards the end, you will learn how to deliver through dialogue as well as design slides.

This book ends with the slide deck in Chapter 5, but have you ever written your pitch starting with the deck? It's not uncommon but it will not help you win funding. As you will discover, the slide deck is the least important part of your pitch.

In order to get the most value from your reading, move through the chapters from start to finish. Key concepts from each chapter build upon each other. This book is intentionally written to be concise so you can move through it quickly. After you're finished, the chapters are divided into subsections with exercises so you can continue using the book as a reference guide for crafting your pitch.

This book is supplemented with additional tools to support you, including the 4-Point Formula sheet. The formula sheet is designed to help you develop your pitch flow and is outlined in Chapter 2. You can download these tools at **pitchpower.org**.

Throughout this book you will also find case studies of successful pitches that model these techniques. Many of these examples were chosen because they're publicly available, giving you the chance to go online and see first-hand how good pitches are performed. Links to these pitches are provided in the back of the book. You can also review detailed analyses of these pitches at **pitchpower.org**.

This book is solely about pitching. There are many other books written on how to find the right investors and navigate the funding process. Such books complement this one; however, no amount of knowing the process will win you investment. A good pitch is how you conquer that first date and build a relationship.

This book is for the thousands of entrepreneurs who have a solid business and are ready to sell it. If you're still at a very early stage of developing your business idea, this book is not for you. Even the best pitch doesn't make a business.[1] However, if you've identified a problem, created a solution for it, and built the framework for a business, continue reading.

You don't need to be a master presenter or persuader to win funding. As you will see from the examples, it simply takes the right techniques applied consciously to capture capital. Whether you're a novice speaker or an expert like me, you will gain effective tools to improve your pitch and increase your chance to win funding.

1 *To build a business, I recommend Steve Blank's The Start-up Owner's Manual*

Audience Focus

Before diving into the formula, there are some ground rules that people without marketing or communication skills must learn. The most important of these skills is to understand your audience. Take a moment now and imagine yourself as an investor:

You did it. After years of hard work, your startup goes public and you walk away with millions. The tables have turned, you're rich, and you're now investing in startups. Entrepreneurs hound you for your autograph as well as your credit card. It's taken years of sweat and blood to earn your money. In what startups will you invest that money? Think about it. The answer isn't difficult. When you listen to entrepreneurs pitch, you only want to know one thing: What's in it for you?

Audiences listen in order to gain value for themselves. During my seven years of presentations coaching and competitive speaking, I never encountered an audience who listened to me for my own sake. Pitches aren't about you or your startup. The goal of your pitch is to communicate what's in it for your audience.

INVESTORS ARE INTERESTED IN FINANCIAL OPPORTUNITIES THAT PRESENT LOW RISK AND HIGH RETURN. Many entrepreneurs speak about themselves and their startup because they believe investors will analyze the product and see an opportunity to make money. This doesn't work. When you leave the interpretation of value up to investors, they might not understand how to translate your startup into financial opportunity. Value is not inherent, it must be expressed. Therefore, frame your pitch to communicate your startup as an investment opportunity with low risk and high return.

This book focuses on pitching to win investment; however, not all investor pitches are geared towards funding. As an entrepreneur, you may be trying to recruit a new advisor or gain additional contacts. If your goal is not funding, consider what's important for your audience to know so they will take the desired action.

In the following chapters, we'll look at how to frame your pitch to fit investor needs. We'll see how Kindara tailored their pitch to inform investors about a unique problem space; how Stormpulse highlighted a lucrative market opportunity; and how DoorDash confirmed they could make money with their business model. In each case the content was about the startup, but the presentation of that content focused on the value to investors.

Clarity

One of the most challenging parts of pitch-writing is clarity. Reid Hoffman, co-founder of LinkedIn and named by *Forbes* as a top 10 tech investor of 2013, emphasized the importance of clarity during an interview: "If I can't get to an investment statement that's statable in … 3-7 bullets, usually I won't invest."

Many entrepreneurs, unclear on how to communicate value, share everything about their startup and fail to communicate anything. Entrepreneurs know their company better than anyone else. This gives a false confidence that they can walk into a meeting and provide all the information an investor needs to make a decision. The problem is that investors don't need a lot of information; they only need the right details to understand the investment opportunity. If an entrepreneur unloads too much information, the important details get lost.

You must decide what content translates clearly into investor value and what content can be eliminated from your pitch. Superfluous details waste investor time and obscure what investors really need to hear in order to make a decision. If you cannot translate product features or company details into signposts that help investors recognize financial opportunity, consider leaving those details out. Hoffman says a good pitch can communicate value in 2 to 3 minutes. Pitch value by pitching tight.

One way to clarify content is to present only the most important information. I recently listened to a VC conversing with a plucky entrepreneur at a startup event. The entrepreneur said he had 20 customers and started to list off names. The VC interrupted to ask simply, "So who's your largest customer?" Notice the VC didn't care about the names of all 20 customers; he only cared about the largest one. When you share details, emphasize only the most important and significant facts. This advice also applies to product description and team details. SHARE ONLY THE MOST IMPRESSIVE AND RELEVANT ELEMENTS DURING YOUR PITCH, AND REMOVE THE LESSER DETAILS TO KEEP YOUR PITCH CONCISE.

When you pitch short and sweet, investors connect to the information they need to determine whether you're investment-worthy. That's all that matters. Conversely, when you add too much detail, in effect dumping everything you know into your pitch, you diminish the impact of your core message. Worse, if you run out of time, you run the risk of never presenting the most valuable information. Amplify your core message and make it crystal clear by reducing the ambient noise.

While the following chapters are dedicated to explaining what content to share and how to deliver that content, clarity cannot be overstated. Simple clear messages are recommended by Dave McClure, founder of the popular incubator 500 Startups; simplicity is highlighted as a necessary technique for effective messaging in the marketing book *Made to Stick* by Stanford Professor Chip Heath and Dan Heath; and simple messages are emphasized for persuasiveness in the book *Lend Me Your Ears,* written by famous speech researcher Max Atkinson. As you craft your pitch, you will discover that clarity takes the most effort. However, it yields a big payoff. Concision is more important than content.

EXERCISE: KEY MESSAGES

Take a moment to consider your startup. When you step in front of investors, WHAT ARE THE THREE MOST IMPORTANT POINTS, THREE KEY TAKE-AWAY MESSAGES THAT INVESTORS MUST KNOW IN ORDER TO RECOGNIZE THE VALUE OF YOUR COMPANY?

To illustrate these key messages, make a short list of data and examples that support each one. (But make sure that the messages are clear even without support.)

1. ....

....

....

2. ....

....

....

3. ....

....

....

Congratulations on completing your first set of exercises! Throughout this book are exercises to help you develop your pitch using various tools and techniques. The exercise set you just completed will help you focus your pitch in the next chapter.

You

Investors don't just listen to what you say, they also pay attention to how you approach problems and perceive opportunities. Heed the words of "super angel" investor David S. Rose, who stated that investors "invest in *you* to make money." Your team is the strongest determinant of startup success, not the product. Investors recognize this, and when you pitch they analyze your knowledge, your skills, and your vision. Rose says he looks in part for integrity, passion, and commitment. Marc Andreessen, one of *Forbes* top 10 investors of 2013, says he aims to find a "trifecta" of traits in people who pitch, including their innovative ability, entrepreneurial spirit, and CEO potential. Whatever the traits, investors are watching more than just words.

It's more important to have solid reasoning behind what you share than have lots of things to share. You will present facts, stories, and other data to support your words when you pitch. The goal of sharing content is not simply to say things, the goal is to say things that make sense. This book provides specific suggestions for content, but you must use your best judgment when selecting the best content for your pitch. Investors assess your reasoning behind the content as much as the content itself. The good news is that when you pitch to investors in a simple clear way, you begin to show that you're a good investment.

In Chapter 3, you will learn how to position your team to enhance credibility. Likewise, Chapter 4 gives you techniques to manage Q&A as well as stand out like a star.

Moving Forward

When you pitch using the guidelines you're about to learn, investors will see you as an effective communicator, team player, and leader. They will want to invest in you. No doubt some of these skills will be familiar to you already. That's because there are thousands of web pages out there machine-gunning opinions at you on how to pitch and making it impossible to distinguish what really matters. This book sorts through the chaos to give you a *complete and integrated* reference source of techniques that are *proven to work.*

Whether you're just starting out, have pitched in meetings but still have no money, or have been told to "come back when you have more traction," this book helps you pitch effectively and win money faster. *More traction* is really code for "you haven't convinced me this is a good investment." Your pitch exists to persuade investors to believe in your business, with or without traction. It takes time and practice to craft a convincing pitch, but when you learn how to pitch well with the techniques in this book, you will significantly enhance your chance to win funding.

FUNDRAISING IS A BRUTAL UNDERTAKING. NOW YOU BEGIN THE JOURNEY TO MEET THIS TOUGH CHALLENGE. THE NEXT TIME YOU STEP INTO AN INVESTOR MEETING WITH THESE TECHNIQUES, YOU ARE FAR MORE LIKELY TO WALK OUT ON THE PATH TO BEING CEO OF THE NEXT MULTI-MILLION DOLLAR START-UP COMPANY.

CHAPTER SUMMARY:

1. Pitch your startup as an investment opportunity with low risk and high return.
2. Emphasize your value as concisely as possible.
3. Note that investors don't just listen to your words, they listen to how you think.

CHAPTER 2

FOUR-POINT PITCH

After watching many of the best and brightest around Silicon Valley, I've identified four critical points of information that you must communicate to investors in order to succeed. These are Problem-Solution-Market-Business.

2. THE FOUR-POINT PITCH

Problem
Solution
Market
Business
Tailoring your pitch
Enigma's pitch

Chapter 2
The Four-Point Pitch

When **Lumier** pitched their desktop tailoring technology in 2011 at TechCrunch Disrupt, it had the makings of a perfect storm. The company had just closed a $350,000 seed round. The buzz was positive as the founder took the stage in front of hundreds of guests. Then he began: "Ah, well ... so, uh, imagine a world of personal computing interfaces tailored to the individual." He painfully shifted to talking about himself: "Umm ... so, ahhh, whom might I be to suggest something like that?" Soon after, he invited the audience to imagine scenarios of missing documents as well as their mother. *Business Insider* later called this pitch "painful to watch." What Lumier's founder needed was a framework.

When you step in front of investors or onstage at TechCrunch Disrupt, the stakes could hardly be higher. You can stumble through your pitch as Lumier did, landing face down. Or you can open floodgates to new funding that sails you to the stars. After watching many of the best and brightest around Silicon Valley, I've identified four critical points of information that you must communicate to investors in order to succeed. These are Problem-Solution-Market-Business.[1]

YOU BEGIN WITH THE PROBLEM, OR THE NEED YOU'RE ADDRESSING. THEN YOU PROCEED TO THE SOLUTION, YOUR PRODUCT OR SERVICE THAT FULFILLS THE NEED. THE MARKET IS THE TARGET CUSTOMERS TO WHOM YOU WILL OFFER YOUR SOLUTION. FINALLY, BUSINESS IS ALL ABOUT THE WAYS YOU'RE GOING TO CAPTURE THAT MARKET.

1 *Famous tech evangelist Robert Scoble also highlights that these points must be addressed to succeed.*

Take a moment to think about the flow of your pitch today. DO YOU BEGIN WITH THE SOLUTION? MANY ENTREPRENEURS DO. Entrepreneurs are focused on their product and often forget the product requires context. When you consider how you arrived at your product, you probably first identified a problem, then after careful consideration created your startup to solve that problem.

Our minds naturally think in terms of problem-solution, and investors' minds work the same.

HUMAN MINDS ARE BIOLOGICALLY PROGRAMMED FOR PROBLEM-SOLUTION THINKING.

This comes from nature as well as nurture. In nature, when we're hungry (problem) we seek food (solution); when we're cold (problem) we seek warmth (solution). In society, we've been nurtured in classrooms to solve problems given to us by teachers. To help your investors understand your product, start with the problem. Once you've delivered a problem, then you can move to your solution.

However, the solution is not where you stop. Your solution benefits people with the problem, it does not benefit investors. Solutions are built to capture markets. Markets help investors realize capital gains from their investments. Therefore, the market is a critical point for investors. After you introduce the market, you must show how you intend to capture that market with your business plan.

Strong pitches are almost always ordered Problem-Solution-Market-Business. Order is critical; it is the logic of your presentation required for the audience to make sense of what you're saying. Order also helps your audience understand the value of your startup. The flow of these points is similar to a good play in baseball. After you hit the ball, you run to first base, then second base, third base, and home before you score. You cannot skip bases or else you're out. First base is your problem, second base is your solution, third base is the market, and home plate is business. If you hit all four bases in order during your pitch, you hit a home run. This chapter explains the overall pitch formula in detail and how to customize your pitch for different investors and industries. Let's play ball!

Problem

You start with the problem to emphasize real-world need and give context to your solution. Great products are successful because people want/need them. The main parts of the problem are the problem description, the pains they cause, and potential trends that lead to a new solution.

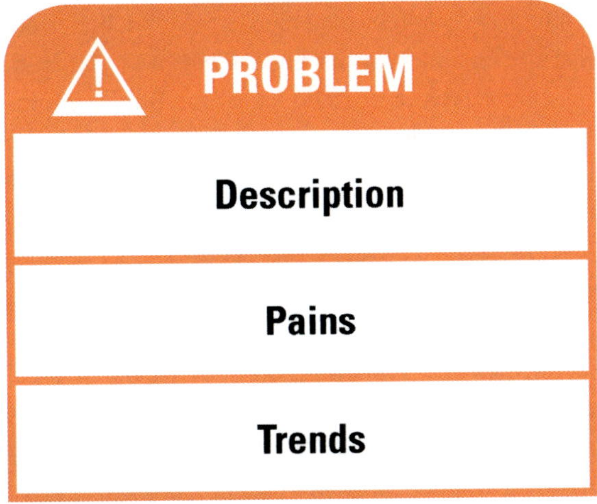

Problem Description

STARTING WITH A CLEAR PROBLEM ORIENTS YOUR AUDIENCE TOWARDS THE SOLUTION BY ENGAGING THEIR NATURAL PROBLEM-SOLUTION THOUGHT PROCESS.

When Lumier pitched TechCrunch Disrupt, the founder spoke all over the place. Not only did the pitch lack clarity, it lacked flow. He never made it to first base. Had he started with a clear description of the problem, he would have oriented his audience towards the solution and given them a chance to figure out the product despite his hesitant words.

When you first introduce the problem, begin with a description so simple your grandma could understand it. Good pitches are clear, concise, and not hyper-technical. Try outlining the problem in 2 to 3 sentences. The more clearly you describe the problem, the easier it will be for investors to engage with your words. Concision is more important than content.

Starting with a clear problem also captures audience interest. When you start with a problem, you introduce a "knowledge gap."[2] A knowledge gap is like a mystery that intrigues audiences and entices them to pay attention. Similar to a story, you introduce a conflict — and now the audience is rooting to get the conflict resolved. Nature and nurture – problems demand solutions.

Just a few months after **Mint.com** closed Series A for their online personal financial service in 2007, founder Aaron Patzer pitched onstage at TechCrunch Top 40. Mint.com would show explosive user growth in what would quickly become half a million users that first year. Could Patzer capture the same attention onstage as his company's product would do online? Patzer started his pitch with a problem. "Is your money working for you?" Patzer outlined briefly the hassles of current finance management tools such as Quicken and Microsoft Money, saying that these tools prevented you from having more money — this was a problem everyone could relate to. But he had a solution. The audience, of course, was hooked!

Mint.com clearly has a great product, but so do many startups. By describing the problem clearly, Patzer was able to effectively capture investor attention and gain an edge over other startups vying for the same capital. After delivering the problem, Patzer cruised through his pitch and won the competition as well as two more rounds of funding before selling Mint.com for $170 million.

2 *Chip Heath and Dan Heath, Made to Stick: Why Some Ideas Survive and Others Die, (New York: Random House, 2007).*

MANY SUCCESSFUL PITCHES ALSO BEGIN THE PROBLEM WITH A SENTENCE OR TWO THAT PROVIDES HIGH-LEVEL CONTEXT ON THE SUBJECT.

For example, if you're introducing a problem in the oil and gas industry, you might begin the problem with a sentence about the importance of oil and gas in today's economy. This high-level view of the subject helps orient investors before you drop into the granular issues.

Finally, when you describe a recognizable problem that people suffer from, you introduce an implicit market at the beginning of your pitch. Investors look for low risk high return. People with problems require solutions. This implicit market attracts investors without requiring you to do a detailed market analysis upfront.

Problem Pains

Problem pains are the consequences to people or businesses with the problem. They may be high costs, inconvenience, or inability to achieve certain goals. The greater the consequences, the more strongly people want a solution. The more people want a solution, the less risk you appear to present as an investment opportunity. In addition, problem pains make your solution look great.

"BETTER, FASTER, CHEAPER" are comparative adjectives that describe your product. Better than what? To show how much better you are compared to the current way of things, introduce problem pains to take advantage of a simple but extremely persuasive technique called contrast.[3]

Contrast, as in the comparison of two items, creates impact. The first item sets the context of value for the second. For example, if I offer you a Dutch chocolate bar for $2, will you buy it? It depends if you're hungry, whether you think $2 is a good deal, etc. Instead, imagine I first told you that Dutch chocolate usually costs $5. Now $2 seems like a great deal. I contrasted $5 against $2, and you might buy my chocolate regardless of your hunger because modern humans are motivated to take advantage of great deals. The price of the chocolate hasn't changed, only the number preceding the price. By deftly introducing the problem before the solution, the $5 candy bar becomes a price hurdle that makes your $2 solution all the sweeter.

In early 2013, I coached an electric car charging company on their technology venture. The company prepares garages in condos for charging electric vehicles. They charge an initial $300 membership fee as well as a monthly fee based on usage. In exchange, the service provides installation management, customer billing, and liability insurance to property management. Using a proprietary power-management technology, the service also scales to allow charging for 6+ vehicles on a single electrical circuit. But how do investors know if this is good?

I had the company start their pitch with the problem pains. Because electrical capacity is limited in most garages and parking spots are far away from residents' electricity meters, condo owners must pay in excess of $10,000 to outfit garages with dedicated electrical circuits to charge their cars. Even if they're willing to pay, many requests to install charging hardware are denied by property management because of installation complexity and liability concerns. In addition, since each dedicated electrical circuit can only charge 1 or 2 vehicles, this process must repeat for every resident with an electric vehicle.

3 Robert Cialdini, *Influence: The Psychology of Persuasion* (HarperBusiness, 2006).

After presenting the problem, the company presented their solution. They compared upfront costs of $10,000 to $300; that's big savings. They also showed that the package of installation management, billing services, and liability insurance mitigated the concerns of property management. Finally, the company showed that whereas a dedicated electrical circuit can charge at most 1 or 2 cars, their brilliant technology allowed 6+ cars to charge from existing circuits within the garage. When the company opened with the problem, they were able to cleanly contrast the pains of the problem with the solution advantages. The team shortly thereafter won first place for best pitch at a startup energy conference.

No Problem? Trends

What if your technology doesn't solve a problem? SOME NEW PRODUCTS ARE SO DISRUPTIVE THEY LITERALLY CHANGE THE WORLD. It seems there's nothing to compare them against. To answer this question, let's look to the most disruptive company of the 21st century, Apple Computer.

When Steve Jobs unveiled the **iPod**, he disrupted the music industry. There was no explicit problem with music per se; rather, consumers often want new cool products to enhance their life. Jobs saw this desire for the newest and coolest as an opportunity. He then introduced a set of *trends* to create context for launching his solution. Let's see if he would have sold you.

Jobs first introduced the iPod by saying that music is a part of everyone's life and people want to carry music around with them wherever they go – a social trend. Music is also going digital with Flash drives and MP3 CDs – a technology trend. However, the cost of carrying digital music using Flash and MP3 CDs is expensive, up to $10 per song in some cases. Conversely, it's much cheaper to store music on hard drives, costing only 30 cents per song – an economic trend. What if there was a way to create a portable music player that stored songs digitally on hard drives? Jobs then introduced the iPod, a device that flowed from the trends and soon become a worldwide bestseller.

Convincing?

If you cannot identify a specific problem, identify trends to set the context for your solution. You can pitch disruptive products by using social, technology, and economic trends. Social trends reflect the behavior of consumers. Technology trends reflect the direction in which technology is moving. Economic trends show paths to price/cost reductions. These trends provide contextual benefits just as if you introduced a problem, but you're free to be as disruptive as the breadth of your ingenuity will allow.

Jobs encored with trend-setting when he introduced the **iPad**. He began by highlighting how smartphones and laptops were being used for web navigation, watching videos, and reading ebooks – social trends. Perhaps there was a way to navigate the web, watch TV, and read ebooks that was better than smartphones or computers, something that fit between them in terms of size – technology trend. Netbooks weren't the answer because they were slow and ran poor software – this set up a contrast. Welcome the iPad.

WHEN YOU HIGHLIGHT TRENDS, YOU ALSO TAKE ADVANTAGE OF THE PERSUASIVE POWER OF SCARCITY.[4]

4 *Noah Goldstein, Steve Martin, & Robert Cialdini, Yes! 50 Scientifically Proven Ways to Be Persuasive (Free Press, 2008).*

Scarcity makes items of limited availability appear more attractive. Retailers use the power of scarcity all the time by offering "limited time" sales that trigger you (and many other buyers) into purchasing products you might otherwise ignore. No one wants to miss a good sale. Likewise, no investor wants to miss an opportunity.

If you position your product through trends, you take advantage of the power of scarcity because you're highlighting an opportunity that won't last forever. This creates time pressure. Trends open up markets, and investors recognize that first-movers who follow trends capture and capitalize those markets.

Problems and trends are not exclusive. Trends signal the direction in which a new product can be developed to solve the current problem. When you identify trends, you can use this powerful concept to transition between the problem (if you've identified one) and the solution. For example, while coaching one entrepreneur who addressed industry quality control, I had him lead with the problem, discuss the problem pains, then highlight trends already taking place in other industries to resolve these pains. This gave him a smooth transition to introduce the trends into his industry.

Problem Wrap-Up

When you start your pitch with a problem (or opportunity), you prepare your audience for the solution by engaging problem-solution thinking. Problems motivate your audience to pay attention to what you say and use the power of contrast to emphasize the benefits of your solution. These advantages give you a necessary edge to win funding and follow your dream.

When **Exactuals** pitched an online payment system for actors in 2011, co-founder and Stanford alum Mike Hurst spent over half his pitch describing the problem of paying royalties and residuals to actors for television shows and films they starred in. Hurst was intimately familiar with the problem; but could he convince investors to put their money into solving a problem they knew nothing about?

Hurst first outlined the problem that every time a television show is rebroadcast, all the actors in the show receive residuals. These payments could be as large as six figures, or as little as 6 cents. Between the studios that initiated the payments, the payroll houses that often cut the checks, and the guilds that processed them, the industry was spending around $5.00 for any given check, even if the check itself was written for $.25. With the ubiquity of electronic payments in today's world, Exactuals was developing a system to replace checks with electronic payments that would save its customers more than 50 percent of their spend while delivering payments five times faster than the existing system.

Hurst started with a clear problem – royalty and residual payments to actors is broken. The problem hooked the audience. By stating the current cost of writing checks at $5.00, Hurst provided a problem pain which he later used to contrast against his much more affordable solution. Finally, Hurst identified the technology trend of electronic payments, allowing him to transition smoothly into his solution. Exactuals quickly closed their seed round which was over-subscribed at $900,000, in part because of Hurst's ability to describe a problem few investors were aware of.

SECTION SUMMARY

1. The problem highlights a real-world need
2. Begin your pitch with a simple problem description to capture investor attention
3. Introduce concrete pains such as higher costs or inconvenience
4. Share social, economic, and technology trends to highlight opportunity

EXERCISE: PROBLEM IDENTIFICATION

1. Write down a problem that people face today (which your product solves). Make it 2 to 3 sentences and so simple that even your grandma would understand it.

2. List concrete pains people with the problem experience (e.g., expensive, inconvenient). How do these pains affect their life? Brainstorm different situations.

3. Identify at least one trend that your solution seems to connect with or express.

4. After you complete the three exercises above, combine them together to describe the problem

Example: Plants frequently die from over-watering. This wastes effort, water and money on dead plants and water bills. With more people using smartphones to manage household activities, maybe there's a way we can solve the problem.

Introducing a clear problem during your pitch is one of the most important steps you can take to winning investment. The exercises above are designed to clarify your thinking.

Solution

Once you round first base, it's time to make for the second. You've primed investors' minds with the problem, and now they're ready to hear your solution. How do you present your solution to reveal greater investment value? You do it by introducing a concise description of your product, a demo, and a list of benefits.

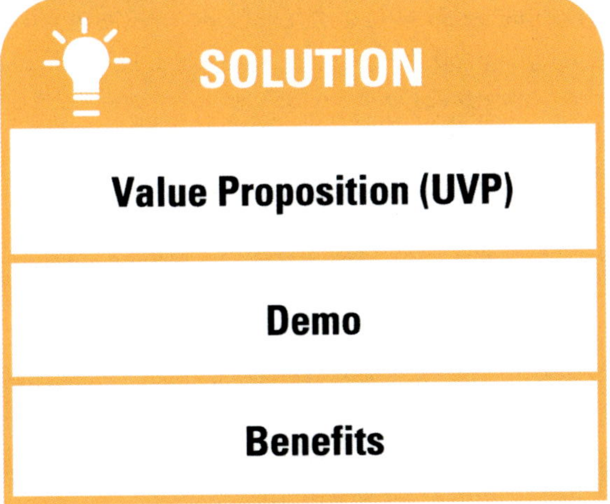

UVP – Your Winning Sentence

When **Loopt** pitched at the 2008 Worldwide Developers Conference, CEO Sam Altman had only two minutes to exhibit Loopt's amazing product. Concision was critical. To succeed, Altman introduced his iPhone app solution with the following words: "Loopt is about connecting with people on the go, which is, after all, the main reason you have a phone. We show you where people are, what they're doing, and what cool places are around you." It took him less than 10 seconds to summarize his product. Altman's simplicity contributed to a great pitch that stood above the crowd, and was perhaps one of the many reasons Loopt was later acquired for $43 million.

GREAT PRODUCT INTRODUCTIONS ARE SHORT AND CLEAR. RESEARCH SHOWS THAT SIMPLE WORDS AND EASY-TO-INTERPRET PHRASES ARE MORE CONVINCING AND MORE LIKABLE.[5]

Altman's simplicity tapped into this persuasive power.

The importance of explaining your product succinctly is so critical that there's a term for it in both marketing and presentation circles. We call it the Unique Value Proposition (UVP). The UVP is a concise statement about what your product does and how it's unique. It is generally one sentence and should be no longer than two sentences. Here are examples of UVPs from some of the hottest startups.[6]

YouTube provides a platform for you to create, connect and discover the world's videos.

Foursquare is a geographical location based social network that incorporates gaming elements.

Mint.com is a free online personal finance service that is aimed at being [an] easy and secure way to manage and save money online.

When you hear a company's UVP, you should understand immediately what the company does. Notice that YouTube, Foursquare, and Mint.com's UVPs include at least one trait about the company that also makes them unique. YouTube allows you to connect and discover. Foursquare includes gaming elements. Mint.com is free, easy, and secure.

5 D.M. Oppenheimer, *Consequences of erudite vernacular utilized irrespective of necessity: Problems with using long words needlessly, Applied Cognitive Psychology, 2006, 20: 139-156*

6 *from Crunchbase.com*

IF YOU WERE TO SUMMARIZE YOUR PRODUCT IN ONE SENTENCE, WHAT WOULD YOU SAY?

Look at the language you use. Many entrepreneurs are eager to disrupt their industries, so they use visionary language to summarize their product such as: *we make it fun to browse the web; our company brings happiness to others; we change the way you do business.* None of these sentences say what the company does because they're not UVPs, they're mission statements. A mission statement is your company's core purpose. Microsoft's mission statement is *"to help people and businesses throughout the world to realize their full potential."* Sounds great, but it doesn't help investors understand the product. It fails the rule of clarity.

AIM FOR UNDERSTANDING. YOU HAVE YOUR ENTIRE SPEECH TO SHARE YOUR MISSION, SO DO NOT LET IT REPLACE YOUR UVP. Avoid verbose language such as: *we are a social gateway to human lifestyle designed to enlist forward-thinking groups by providing culinary acidic experiences.* Better to simply say: *we're a coffeehouse for entrepreneurs.*

You might have read online about using taglines to describe your business such as the "Facebook for retired people" or "Craigslist for free stuff." Using short statements like these can convey a lot of meaning in a little package; however, not all investors are drawn to this approach.[7] Many now-funded companies used taglines to elucidate the product, but they did so *after* delivering the UVP. The taglines added clarity and understanding to their UVP without substituting for it.

Finally, I've met many entrepreneurs who face the challenge of having a product do too many things. The worst thing a product can do is "everything," because a product that does everything solves nothing. Focus your company's message by creating a UVP. When you deliver your UVP well, you'll shine as **Badgeville** did at TechCrunch Disrupt.

In 2011, co-founder Kris Duggan started Badgeville's pitch by explaining the trend of using web tools to drive user engagement on company websites. Duggin highlighted the problem that only a few companies have access to these tools, and he asserted that the tools should be available to all companies. Duggan then delivered Badgeville's UVP: "We're a loyalty and rewards platform for web publishers to drive engagement." The UVP was clear, concise, and directly resolved the problem. As of today, Badgeville has raised nearly $40 million. They have a solid business, and their UVP helped them communicate that business to investors.

Demo – Show and Tell

After you deliver the UVP, it's time to show your product. The emphasis here is to *show* versus *tell*. Investors often want to see products, not hear about products. One great way to do this is to run through your demo as a hypothetical user. After Loopt delivered their UVP, CEO Altman demoed Loopt by going through a real-world situation of using the app to find a nearby friend. As he searched for his friend, he showed off the map interface. Once he located the friend, Altman showed more features oriented around peer-to-peer interaction. He introduced a hypothetical action, "I don't have lunch plans today, so we'll see if she's free," and showed that he could call or text his friend, expounding that these product features integrated smoothly with the phone.

7 *In the popular marketing book Made to Stick, authors Heath and Heath affirm that taglines are effective at making your message clear and sticky in the minds of investors; conversely, Digg co-founder and Google Ventures partner Kevin Rose suggested that he doesn't invest in companies which mimic others (as inferred through the use of taglines)*

The demo made perfect sense from a user standpoint and allowed Altman to unabashedly show off his cool technology. Through each step of the process, Altman expanded on the features in the app such as the map interface, communication functions, and peer-to-peer information.

WHEN YOU SHOW YOUR PRODUCT, EXPLAIN IT FROM THE STANDPOINT OF A HYPOTHETICAL USER. By taking a user's perspective, the demo relates more to your audience. Research suggests that the easier it is for your audience to imagine using your product, the more positively they evaluate your product.[8] What type of hypothetical user should you choose? Choose a user who suffers from the problem, and then show how your product solves that user's particular problem.

To make your demo even easier to relate to, explain product features using familiar descriptions. When Steve Jobs introduced the iPod, he didn't focus on the fact that iPod has five gigabytes of memory, he noted that it holds 1,000 songs. Five gigabytes of memory to a non-technical audience is meaningless, whereas 1,000 songs are meaningful. The iPod isn't just 4 inches by 2 inches in size; it's the size of a deck of cards. Relatable terms make it easy for your audience to grasp the product.

AS YOU LEAD INVESTORS THROUGH THE FEATURES, THIS IS YOUR OPPORTUNITY TO CONTRAST PRODUCT FEATURES WITH PROBLEM PAINS. Jobs did this when he introduced Firewire as a fast way to transfer songs to the iPod. Whereas previous MP3 players using USB required 5 hours to load 1,000 songs, Firewire takes less than 10 minutes to transfer songs to the iPod. The contrast between 5 hours and 10 minutes showed Firewire to be a powerful feature. When you contrast problem pains with solution features, investors gain a clearer understanding of how your solution solves the problem.

Altman took the risk of presenting a live demo, but I've seen live demos fail completely when Internet connection is lost or the product hits a bug. When the demo fails, your pitch fails. A safer option is to record your demo and play it back for your audience. Perhaps better yet, run a live demo with a backup recording. This way if the Internet goes down, you can use the recording rather than watch your pitch swirl into the abyss.

What if you can't demo because the demo doesn't fit a meeting room environment? Show your solution through pictures and screenshots; share examples of the solution in action. When I coached a graduate student at Stanford on his website design service, he used before-and-after screenshots to illustrate how his product redesigned company web portals to attract more visitors. The critical takeaway is *show* versus *tell*.

What if you can't demo because you don't have a product? Show a minimal viable product, often referred to as an MVP. An MVP is a prototype, your working example of the product with minimal features that address the problem. Having an MVP is so important that investor and influencer Guy Kawasaki emphasizes he would rather see a prototype without a pitch than a pitch without a prototype, in part be-

8 W.L. Gregory, R.B. Cialdini, and K.M. Carpentar, *Self-relevant scenarios as mediators of likelihood estimates and compliance: does imagining make it so? Journal of Personality and Social Psychology, 1982, 43: 89-99; P.K. Petrova and R.B. Cialdini, Fluency of consumption imagery and the backfire effects of imagery appeals, Journal of Consumer Research, 2005, 32:442-452; and N. Mandel, P.K. Petrova, and R.B. Cialdini, Images of success and the preference for luxury brands. Journal of Consumer Psychology, 2006, 16(1): 57-69*

cause a prototype "significantly reduce[s] one risk, which is that you can actually deliver a product." Remember investors look for low risk high return.

What if you need investment before you can build a product? Show you can build it. I once watched a group of entrepreneurs pitch noise-cancellation technology for vehicles. The team needed investment to purchase hardware for development. After the pitch, investors said they loved the idea but wanted to see proof that the team could develop it. One way these entrepreneurs could have shown proof would have been to run tests showing they could build noise-cancellation technology on a small scale. Again, investors need to see something. Let them see their risk is low because the product's viability is high.

Benefits Sell

To encourage further investor buy-in, never forget the golden rule of sales: FEATURES TELL WHILE BENEFITS SELL. Features are what you put into your product; benefits are what those features mean to users. Benefits win customers and ultimately investors.

Selling benefits means you explain features of your solution in terms of user value or experience. When Steve Jobs introduced the first iPod with 20-minute skip protection (feature), he said you can go running or do other exercise without missing a beat (benefit). The iPod holds 1,000 songs (feature) so you can take your entire music library with you when you go on vacation (benefit).

Benefits translate product features into meaningful value. Failure to translate features into benefits is a frequent mistake entrepreneurs make when pitching their product. Stand out from the pack. Don't leave it up to investors to guess the value, tell them.

Solution Wrap-Up

When you deliver your UVP and demo while sharing benefits, it often becomes unnecessary to explain *how* your product works. You've given everything investors need to link your solution to the problem and show low risk high return. Some entrepreneurs waste time with in-depth discussions of back-end technology, etc. Entrepreneurs do this because they don't understand their own product benefits and hope investors will figure them out if they explain the details. Don't fall into this trap. You're there to win funding, not to get a good grade on a college exam. Stick with simplicity and you're on the right track.

When **ZocDoc**'s founders pitched "an online way to book doctor and dentist appointments" at TechCrunch40 in 2007, CEO Cyrus Massoumi and COO Oliver Kharraz, MD, faced an investor panel that included Guy Kawasaki. Kawasaki is known for his wisdom as well as his strong opinions. To succeed under this pressure, Massoumi and Kharraz didn't explain how their technology worked, they showed it.

After introducing the problem and delivering ZocDoc's UVP, the founders demoed the product twice while listing off benefits. In the process of searching for a doctor, Kharraz explained that you have all the information necessary to make an appointment (feature), and if you book an appointment online, you don't need to wait when you arrive in the office (benefit). He introduced a hypothetical situation where you break your tooth and need an emergency dentist appointment. The example was relatable to the audience and made it easy to follow along. Kharraz went through the process a customer would go through in the same situation – locating a nearby doctor, filtering by insurances accepted, reading verified reviews and then booking the appointment (features). Then he translated these features into a benefit by showing how quick the process of making an appointment can be during an emergency. Massoumi ended the demo by listing off other use cases, ensuring further audience relatability.

After the pitch concluded, Kawasaki shared his doubts about the product. However, the pitch was so successful that co-panelist and angel investor Esther Dyson sided with the startup to challenge Kawasaki's doubts. In 2011, just four years after their appearance at TechCrunch, ZocDoc closed Series C with $75 million.

SECTION SUMMARY

1. The solution shows your product or service
2. Start your solution with a single-sentence UVP of what you do and why you're unique
3. Demo your product through the experience of a hypothetical customer
4. Translate product features into explicit customer benefits

EXERCISE: SOLUTION ORGANIZATION

1. Create a 1-2 sentence UVP for your company. Ensure your UVP explains what your company does and includes at least one trait that makes your company unique. When you're finished, test it on an acquaintance who doesn't know what you do. If they still don't understand what you do after sharing your UVP, revise and repeat.

2. Identify a situation in which a hypothetical customer with the problem uses your solution. Walk through the ways they use your solution to solve their problem. Go into specific details.

3. Use the chart below to list out problem pains you listed in the previous exercise set. Next to each pain, list a feature of your solution that solves the pain. Next to each feature, write a concrete benefit to the customer.

PROBLEM PAINS	SOLUTION FEATURES	SOLUTION BENEFITS
ex. $2000 installation	$300 installation	Anyone can afford

4. Go back to the situation you created for your demo. As you walk through a customer using your solution, highlight a benefit every time you show off a new feature.

How do you feel about your product explanation now? The goal of this exercise is to describe your product concisely and provide benefits to your audience.

Market

You've made it around two bases on the baseball field. Time to head for the third.

INVESTORS INVEST FOR ONE PRIMARY REASON: TO EARN MONEY. YOUR SOLUTION DOESN'T SHOW FINANCIAL OPPORTUNITY PER SE, BUT YOUR MARKET DOES. MARKET IS THE POTENTIAL CUSTOMER BASE FOR YOUR SOLUTION.

When **Stormpulse** CEO Matt Wensing pitched at Capital Factory Demo Day in 2011, he had only 3 minutes to woo investors with his weather tracking system for businesses. Wensing knew that weather problems are so obvious that they border on the banal, and Wensing's solution, while elegant, was no more exciting than meteorological subjects usually turn out to be. Could Wensing's pitch really appeal to investors?

In his 3-minute pitch, Wensing spent 26 seconds on the problem and solution. 26 seconds! He rounded first and second base so fast you could see dust flying up behind his heels. Wensing realized that weather and weather tracking systems are straightforward, so there was no need to discuss them in-depth. After this crisp problem-solution explanation, he spent the next two and a half minutes discussing his market. He shared stories about customers who had reached out to Stormpulse, including Apple, FedEx, and The White House. Not all of these customers had enrolled in his service, but their interest in Stormpulse confirmed a strong market. Notice that Wensing also showed off his best customers and ignored talking about little ones. When investors hear that the United States White House is interested in your product, there's no doubt about financial opportunity.

Most startups can't show off their market by listing major customer interest as Stormpulse did, but you can rely on the basic marketing standards outlined in MBA textbooks. Entrepreneurs tend to immediately think of market size when they consider their market, but size is just one factor. Your goal is to introduce your market in such a way that it emphasizes low risk high return. You do this by targeting your market, measuring the size, and showing you can seize it.

Target

Before you can begin discussing the size of your market, you must identify your market. There's a universe of markets waiting for your product; you decide who the first lucky customers are. You can target an existing market, segments of an existing market, or even a new market. For example, if you were to create a new web browser, would you go after customers using it for business, education, or recreation? If you've done your homework, you've already decided your market and now you just need to pitch it.

Pitching your market means knowing your market – who are the customers and what are their needs. This description of potential customers is your market. The goal of targeting is accuracy. The clearer the bull's-eye, the more accurately you can hit the target.

Take a moment to consider your market. How well do you know your target customers? When considering who these customers are, try to imagine specific details. Consider their age, gender, lifestyle, daily activities. In essence, see if you can create a *day in the life of* story for a typical customer so as to visualize exactly who they are and how they live. In The Startup Owner's Manual, authors Steve Blank and Bob Dorf write that a day in the life of story is "one of the most powerful ways to understand your customers." Accuracy first.

Size

Once you've identified the market, you can focus on size. Size is how you show investors high return. To show size, you need to measure your market.

You can measure your market top-down or bottom-up. Top-down is a process of elimination that begins with essentially everybody who could possibly purchase your product and then slowly narrows the focus by magnifying down to a certain point. For example, if you have a new iPhone app, you might start with everyone in the industry who has an iPhone, and then focus on everyone you can reach through your current marketing and distribution channels, etc. Some professionals call this the TAM-SAM-SOM approach. However, in my interview with Angel Investor Russ Siegelman, he recommended using the bottom-up approach.

Bottom-up targets specific customers you can reach now, then widens the lens to include more customers you can reach at later stages of growth. We might imagine that Mark Zuckerberg used the bottom-up approach when pitching Facebook to investors. For example, his initial market was Harvard students. He might then have expanded his market to include Ivy League universities, then more universities, the families of students at universities, etc. The benefit of this approach is that you focus on the immediate market first and spend less time considering pie-in-the-sky numbers.

By measuring top-down or bottom-up, you quantify the size of your initial market and show a scalable path of growth to larger financial opportunity. This initial market size along with a vision of scale attracts investors with the potential for high return. Some entrepreneurs even use both top-down and bottom-up to ensure further accuracy in their measurements.

AT THE END OF THE DAY, GETTING OFF THE GROUND INTO A SMALL BUT WELL-DEFINED MARKET IS MORE IMPORTANT THAN ATTEMPTING TO PIERCE A LARGE MARKET. This requires accuracy. Many investors prefer bottom-up measurements precisely because this requires entrepreneurs to focus accurately on the immediate market, whereas top-down measurements are frequently inflated by at least 2-3x the real market size. Accuracy also applies to your vision of scale. Angel investor David S. Rose highlights "realism" as one of the top 10 qualities he looks for in entrepreneurs, so be real in your market assessment.

Seizure - Advantages

No matter the accuracy or size of your market, do you have the capability to go after that market? To go after a market, you must show how you differentiate your own enterprise from the competition and whether you have the capability to engage and acquire customers. Your goal is to lower the perceived risk for investors that you can enter the market successfully.

Appconomy was chugging along with a solid $1.5 million Series A when the CEO pitched their new iPhone app at a launch conference in early 2011. The new app allowed friends and colleagues to communicate in groups across multiple platforms. The market was potentially huge. During Q&A, the CEO got a zinger of a question from one VC panelist, asking how his app differed from Facebook groups. The CEO's response seemed to confuse the panelist. The next panelist asked again how they differentiated from other companies in the online social space. As the session was closing, the panelists appeared unconvinced that Appconomy could seize their target market from the other options out there. The conference organizer then commented the pitch was becoming a "train wreck."

TO DIFFERENTIATE FROM YOUR COMPETITION, SHARE UNIQUE QUALITIES OF YOUR COMPANY SUCH AS FEATURES, SERVICES, OR PRICING.

Perhaps you have a feature that makes your product easier for consumers to use. Maybe you offer stellar service when supporting customers. Perhaps you provide the product at a lower price by focusing on cost leadership through operational efficiencies.[9]

The purpose of differentiation is to explain how you have a competitive advantage in the marketplace. Competitive advantage is not necessarily obvious. For example, lower price doesn't necessarily provide an advantage: if you're introducing a new wine to the wine industry, lower prices might harm your business. Therefore, be explicit in stating how your differentiation is likely to win customers. Finally, heed the words of LinkedIn co-founder and VC Reid Hoffman: "If you can't articulate your competitive advantage in a simple way, you don't have one."

Competition is not the only barrier affecting your ability to seize a market. You may need to show your company has the ability to engage and acquire customers in the market. I've coached entrepreneurs who pitch solutions for third-world economies in Africa. Before these products reach the market, it's very likely they will encounter language barriers. Likewise, in order to acquire customers in such a market, the entrepreneurs need to have access to the right distribution channels and ensure they can manage government compliance. Take time to consider anything that affects your ability to seize the market. When you show investors you can seize the market, you lower the risk of investment.

Market Wrap-Up

When you target, size, and show you can seize your market, investors see you're serious. Stormpulse did this in one smooth sweep by highlighting the interest of potential customers, and they have since raised over $2 million. In the next chapter, you'll discover ways to enhance the presentation of your market details.

When you introduce your market skillfully, investors want to know more about your business. Just as a problem creates a "knowledge gap" that hooks investors into listening for a solution, a tantalizing market creates an "opportunity gap" that hooks investors into hearing how you're going to capture that market.

9 Investor Steve Ciesinski suggests that smaller companies may sometimes be more threatening than larger companies. If you face large competitors, you can position yourself as having an advantage by being more nimble and capable of responding to the market faster. Conversely, small startups share many of the advantages you inherently possess

SECTION SUMMARY

1. The market is the customer base you can reach today
2. Be as detailed as possible in describing your target customers (age, lifestyle, etc.)
3. Measure your current market size using top-down or bottom-up approaches
4. Explain your competitive advantage over other solutions on the market

EXERCISE: MARKET POSITION

1. Identify the traits of your target customers. What are their age range, lifestyle, and needs? Wrap these details into a day-in-the-life of a customer story.

2. Estimate the size of the market using either top-down or bottom-up measurement.

3. Create a competitive comparison chart. List your product features and any other differentiators in the left column, and then confirm whether these features are in your competitors' products. Wherever you list a feature that is not used by the competition, explain how your feature provides a competitive advantage to winning customers.

FEATURE	COMPETITOR 1	COMPETITOR 2	YOUR SOLUTION
Multi-car charging	✗	✗	✓

It's important to know your market regardless of whether you're pitching or running a business. These exercises help clarify who are you customers.

Business

After you've identified a market, it's time to describe *how* you're going to capture that market. This is your business plan. When **CrowdFanatic** pitched their peer-to-peer confrontation website on *Shark Tank* (I admit I occasionally watch), the founder concluded his pitch by saying the site earns revenue through a "targeted marketing" strategy. That was it. He then suffered four minutes of imprecations from investors. Without a proper revenue model, they called his plan the "worst path to making money I've ever heard" and a "bad presentation."

STARTUPS ARE MORE THAN PRODUCTS, THEY'RE BUSINESSES.

Many entrepreneurs are familiar with Alexander Osterwalder's Business Model Canvas used to outline a business model. If you've completed the Business Canvas, most of what you've written goes here. You don't want to be stuck in CrowdFanatic's shoes, disparaged on national television for failing to think about business. You rounded three bases successfully, but you don't score until you touch home plate. This is home plate.

The business plan is made up of two parts: your go-to-market strategy and your revenue model. The two are interrelated, but we'll look at them independently. We'll then look at how you finish your pitch by presenting company milestones.

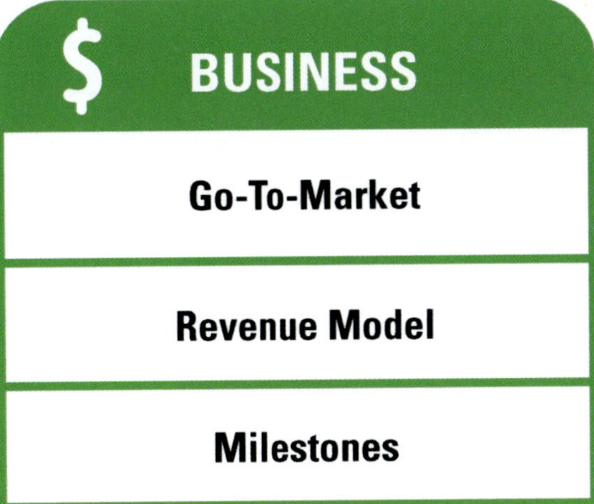

Go-to-Market Strategy

Go-to-market strategy is how you get, keep, and grow customers. When modeling how you get customers, you might discuss marketing, distribution channels, partnerships, and how you leverage your competitive advantages and pricing strategy. Some entrepreneurs dodge this step by saying they'll use viral marketing to acquire customers. If so tempted, heed the words of Guy Kawasaki: "Viral marketing is the equivalent of saying that your strategy is 'to get lucky.'" If investors want to get lucky with their cash, they go to Vegas; they don't invest in startups.

After you acquire customers, outline how you intend to keep customers. It's been said that the cost of acquiring customers is 10 times the cost of retaining customers, so investors may be interested to know how you manage customers after you win them over. Some ways to keep customers are loyalty programs, events, and incentives that drive engagement. United Airlines provides a frequent flyer program to retain customers, and as a result I've been a loyal United flyer for almost a decade.

Finally, explain how you intend to grow the customer base from your existing customers. Common models to expand your customer base include referral programs and incentives that drive sharing through social networks. When Dropbox came out, my friends petitioned me relentlessly to open a Drobox account because they would get additional online space for every new friend they referred. Part of Dropbox's success can certainly be attributed to their referral model.

WHEN YOU PITCH HOW TO GET, KEEP, AND GROW CUSTOMERS, YOU NEED TO SHOW MORE THAN JUST MODELS. A PITCH REQUIRES PROOF.

Therefore, deliver your go-to-market strategy by first introducing the models and then showing proof that your models work. The next chapter will look more at proof.

Revenue Model

When you outline how you bring your product to market, you must also explain how you monetize your product. Investors are interested in high return, and you need to show return through revenue. To pitch your revenue model, introduce your revenue strategy and then show costs, pricing, and sales. Examples of revenue strategies (in the online industry) include freemium, subscription, and ad-funded strategies.

When RidePal CEO Nathalie Criou pitched her revenue model for a bus service to carry commuters from San Francisco to south Silicon Valley, she had to contend with what she self-described as "the one industry where you don't make money." She focused her revenue stream on commuter transportation from San Francisco to the south end of Silicon Valley, her core service. She shared that her strategy was to rent seats on RidePal buses to companies. Criou then compared the costs of renting buses from a third-party company with the price RidePal charged for seats, confirming a healthy gross margin of 60 percent. Shortly after this pitch, RidePal won $500,000 in seed funding.

When you pitch your revenue model, choose one primary revenue stream to focus on and stick to it. Many entrepreneurs go into great detail about multiple revenue streams, hoping to boost ROI estimates. If you show too many ways to make money, it might come across as though you're not exactly sure how to make money. Likewise, the more revenue streams you present in your pitch, the more you leave yourself vulnerable to doubt. If even one of the revenue streams you depend on appears dubious, it can reflect back and make all your revenue streams appear dubious.

To make your company appear more lucrative, how can you discuss multiple revenue opportunities without raising doubts? Here's how RidePal did it: Criou focused her description on one stream as the source of her revenue. Criou later mentioned that premium services could be offered, which could perhaps double the revenue. This made her model even more lucrative. However, she avoided going into details about these services. This additional revenue stream was a future opportunity, not the core business focus. Her success didn't depend on additional revenue streams, it depended on her core business only. By emphasizing her main stream, Criou ensured that the additional streams were visible but the risks associated with them would not reflect back on her solid core assumptions.

The revenue model helps investors recognize high return; as a result, many startups believe the revenue model must show revenue predictions that exceed the wildest dreams of investors. In fact, VCs suggest the opposite – Marc Andreessen, one of Forbes' 2013 top 10 venture capitalists, recommends you avoid creating a "financial plan that is designed to appeal to the investor," and instead create a "financial plan that you believe." Likewise, some investors prefer *cost* estimates over *revenue* predictions. Revenue is difficult to predict (at best) and often inflated by optimism; whereas a good business knows its costs.

Despite the inclination of many entrepreneurs to display spreadsheets of data, keep your revenue model simple. Your revenue model is not a lesson in spreadsheet mathematics. Be able to talk about your revenue strategy and expense structure, but keep the full financials to paper that can be shared post-pitch. Criou showed RidePal's revenue and costs on a single slide without details. During your pitch, the goal is to convey that you have a clear revenue model, not a detailed one. If investors want to dive into spreadsheet mathematics, invite them to have a follow-up meeting.

Milestones

Now we come to the purpose of your pitch – investment. Your go-to-market strategy and revenue model demonstrate you can do business. Finish your pitch by bringing them together to show milestones achieved and future milestones over the next 18 months. This is the summary of your business-to-date and where you're heading. Why only 18 months? Because you're a startup, and a lot will change in 18 months.

Milestones are critical. First, you show that you're already on a path towards success by highlighting your achievements. Second, if you're going to ask for money, you must explain where that money will go. Future milestones help you do this. If your family won't lend you money without an explanation of how you're going to use it, there's little chance an investor will part with serious dough if they don't know where it's going.

WHEN YOU TAKE TIME TO HIGHLIGHT FUTURE MILESTONES AND HOW INVESTMENT WILL BE SPENT ACHIEVING THESE GOALS, YOU GIVE YOURSELF THE POWER TO NEGOTIATE.

If you win funding, investors won't necessarily want to give you the amount you ask. They might offer only half of what you ask. To negotiate, you can explain how different levels of funding contribute to different levels of growth in your business. You might well survive on half of the investment; but the more you get, the faster you build the business, achieve your milestones, and earn them return on their investment.

When you ask for money, it also helps to show what investments you already have and engage the power of social proof.[10] According to research, people are more likely to do what other people do. If you share that you have funding from other investors, particularly well-established ones, then your current audience is more likely to follow suit and invest in you as well. If you don't have outside money but have invested a significant portion of your own personal finances into the startup, share your personal investment. Person-

10 Noah Goldstein, Steve Martin, & Robert Cialdini, Yes! 50 Scientifically Proven Ways to Be Persuasive (Free Press, 2008).

al investment demonstrates your passion and commitment to making the company a success.

HOW YOU ASK FOR MONEY ALSO HAS AN EFFECT ON WHAT YOU RECEIVE.

There's no reason not to ask for cash straight-up. In fact, Peter Thiel, one of Forbes top 10 VCs, recommends you have a clear ask. But there are other skillful ways to slip the question. Doximity CEO and co-founder Jeff Tangney, who successfully breezed through his seed round, shared the following advice based on his experience: "If you ask for money, investors will give you advice. If you ask for advice, they'll give you money."

Another skillful way I've seen to ask for cash is to stick with the basic principle of audience focus. Rather than say, "We want you to give us $1 million," which sounds selfish and focuses on you rather than what's in it for the investors, say it the way IPO roadshow coach and presentations author Jerry Weissman suggests: "We invite you to share in this opportunity."

Finally, you might be asked about your exit strategy. Focusing on a long-term goal of acquisition or IPO can help you make strategic decisions; however, exit strategy should not be a focus of your pitch.[11] If investors ask about your exit strategy, they could be looking to turn your company around for a quick profit. If that's the case, maybe they're not the right partners for you.[12]

Business Wrap-Up

Business is how you plan to capture the market and earn revenue. You do this by presenting your go-to-market strategy and revenue model. VC Reid Hoffman shared that in his experience, complex business plans fail. As a founder, it may be tempting to deep-dive into the complex details of your business plan. Don't. When you present business, your goal is to convince investors you have a clean way to capture the market and generate profit. Make your pitch straightforward and clear.

11 Lightspeed Ventures partner Arif Janmohamed considers discussions on exit stage to be one of the 5 ways to ensure you won't get funded. The other 4 are requesting an NDA, thinking too small, asking for a term sheet prior to due diligence, and focusing too strongly on valuation.

12 David Ladd, former managing director at Mayfield, mentioned that the right way to respond to inquiries about exit strategy is to say: "My plan is to build a fast-growing profitable company. And then see, if the public markets [go] there, I'll go there ... and if [sic] not, I think one of these three guys will be interested in me."

SECTION SUMMARY

1. Business is how you bring your solution to market and make money

2. Introduce go-to-market strategy to explain how you get, keep, and grow your customer base

3. Present a revenue model to show how you monetize from going to market

4. List out past and future milestones to show accomplishments and where you're heading

EXERCISE: BUSINESS PLAN

Many startups use the Business Model Canvas created by Alexander Osterwalder to outline their business plan. Note that seven of the nine boxes on the canvas fit smoothly into the business portion of your pitch:

1. Key Partners – Business
2. Key Activities – Business
3. Key Resources – Business
4. Customer Relationships – Business
5. Channels – Business
6. Cost Structure – Business
7. Revenue Streams – Business
8. Value Proposition – Solution, Market
9. Customer Segments – Market

Complete the Business Model Canvas.

Completing the business model allows you to answer the following two questions: how do you capture the market? How do you make money while capturing the market?

Tailoring Your Pitch

When you round all four bases in sequential order, Problem-Solution-Market-Business, you score a home run. This is the 4-Point Pitch. The order is important because you can't capture the market without first knowing the market; you can't move into the market until you have a solution to bring to market; and you can't have a solution until you have a problem you're solving.

Not all pitches are the same, and not all points are equally important to your pitch. Exactuals delivered the problem through almost half of their 15-minute pitch. Conversely, Stormpulse delivered their problem and solution in 26 seconds over a 3-minute pitch. Great pitches I've seen center around two or three points and downplay the others. How do you decide which points to focus on? There's no hard rule, so focus on two aspects: know your audience and know your strengths.

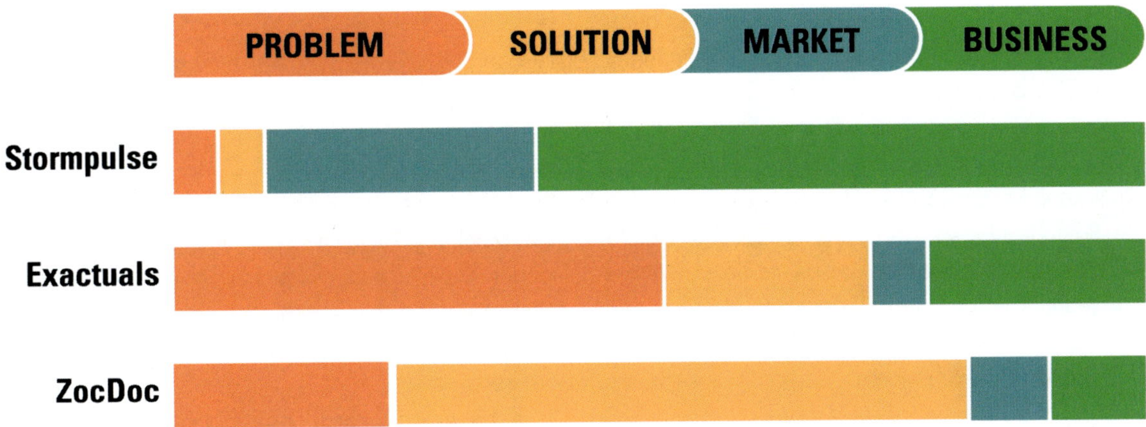

Know Your Audience

Investors have different levels of knowledge; spend time pitching details that are unfamiliar to investors. This could include an obscure problem, a unique solution, an untapped market, or a stellar business plan. When Exactuals pitched their now-oversubscribed seed round, most investors were unfamiliar with how Hollywood actors are paid, so CEO Hurst spent time outlining the problem in depth. When Stormpulse pitched weather-reporting technology to investors, the problem and solution were so obvious that CEO Wensing spent little time on them – what made the company lucrative to investors was the market. Exactuals and Stormpulse are examples of tailoring the pitch to the audience.

Similarly, identify where the highest investment risks are and focus on reducing those risks. For example, if the primary risk is developing the technology, spend more time discussing the solution. If the primary risk is market risk, spend more time explaining the market and business.

Consider focusing also on what makes you unique and more successful than the 10 other companies who might be pitching similar ideas to yours. When I interviewed angel investor and SRI executive Steve Ciesinski, he said it's not uncommon that he'll be pitched three times a day! As a result of the sheer volume, he and other investors might hear identical pitches from 5, 10, even 20 startups. This makes investors knowledgeable often about your problem, solution, and even your market. Focus on your uniqueness. Does your product have exciting benefits, do you have a powerful competitive advantage, is your business plan robust?

Angel investors also differ from VCs. If you're pitching to angels, the emphasis for investors is often the problem and the team, not necessarily the solution or the business. Solutions can change in a young startup; hence the popularity of the word "pivot." Likewise, the business plan of a young startup is frequently undeveloped. Therefore, angels may look to a viable problem area that can be addressed with a solid team. Contrast angels to VCs who may analyze your startup to see whether you have a robust product and a viable business model.

Know Your Strengths

When you know your strengths and weaknesses, you can tailor your pitch to put your best foot forward. For example, after reading this chapter you might discover that you have a clear problem and solution but you haven't yet clearly identified the market. Of course you will now go out and identify the market so you can pitch effectively; but your next pitch is in a week. You don't have time.

Instead of showing broad imaginary market numbers during your pitch such as the total number of iPhone users, you could focus your pitch on describing the problem and solution. When it comes time to discuss the market, be very brief and re-emphasize that the ubiquity of the problem and the time you've spent creating an amazing solution are likely to yield a large market. After all, if you aren't clear on your market because you've put time into creating a great solution, that's not bad. But showing a make-believe market is not good.

FOCUS ON YOUR STRENGTHS BY GIVING THEM THE MOST AIRTIME. If you developed an amazing product but haven't taken steps to identify your market or bring your product to market yet, spend more time on the solution and less time talking about the market and business. This puts your best qualities forward, and you also convey to the audience that your strengths are the most important aspect of your startup. Research suggests the time you spend on one point of your pitch versus another will make the longer aspect seem more important.[13] After you move through the next chapter, you'll better understand where your strengths reside.

In 2013 at TechCrunch Disrupt NYC, **Enigma** took the stage to pitch how they make public data easily accessible on the Internet. The company had just received over $1 million in seed funding, but communicating the complexities of public data is difficult at best. The murmur of the crowd subsided as co-founders Marc DaCosta and Hicham Oudghiri began speaking. DaCosta started with the problem and detailed the pains of current public data access, including data inaccessibility and unwieldy search. He then presented a succinct UVP of Enigma as the solution to these problems. Oudghiri stepped in to

13 Z. L. Tormala and R. E. Petty, Contextual contrast and perceived knowledge: Exploring the implications for persuasion, Journal of Experimental Social Psychology, 2007, 43: 17-30

demo the product, accessing data from Google and Facebook to make the demo relatable and interesting to the audience. Oudghiri concluded the pitch with a short show of major partnerships between Harvard Business School and the New York Times. The pitch was problem-solution focused, downplaying the market and business, and the co-founders stunned the audience. They finished their pitch to roaring applause.

The first comments from the judges' panel were "great," "awesome job," and "one of the best presentations I've seen." The judges still asked questions about the market and revenue model; however, DaCosta and Oudghiri set the hook of interest so powerfully with their description of the problem and solution that they ended up winning the grand prize of $50,000.

SECTION SUMMARY:

1. Pitches are often tailored to emphasize two or three points
2. Focus on pitch points that facilitate the audience's understanding and interests
3. Bring attention to those points in your pitch that highlight your startup's strengths

EXERCISE: PRIMARY POINTS

1. Identify which points might be new to investors by considering the questions below:
   - Is the problem obvious or is it relatively unknown?
   - Is your solution straightforward or extremely unique?
   - Has the market been identified or is it new?
   - Can your strategy be easily executed, or do you have a novel approach?

2. Consider your knowledge around each of the four points. Rank each point according to how effectively you can discuss it, ordering from most effectively to least effectively.

3. Last chapter you completed an exercise identifying the three messages investors must know in order to recognize your company value. Identify which points each of these messages belong to.

4. Review your answers to the previous three questions. Now that you've identified the needs of investors, your strengths, and the must-knows, label two points that will maximize the effectiveness of your pitch.

When you know the most important points of your pitch, you can craft a pitch for any circumstance by focusing on these points. Whether presenting for 2 minutes or 20 minutes, use your discoveries in the exercises above to focus on the areas that count.

Conclusion

You now have a formula of 4 points for your startup pitch. Like baseball, when you round all 4 bases successfully, you score. In a pitch, the same rules apply. During your main presentation, you might move through some bases faster than others. However, investors will eventually ask you to address all 4 points during discussion, so be prepared.

To help you design your pitch, use the 4-Point Pitch Formula worksheet available for download at **pitchpower.org**.

Many presentations coaches recommend you have a clear overarching story and message during your pitch. This formula is your overarching story: There is a problem you're solving that provides a magnificent business opportunity. Your message is clear: because you have a stellar solution, a major market, and/or a great business plan, investors need to invest in you to take advantage of the value you present.

Content comes next – what are the specific details you can show to make your formula persuasive. You'll find answers on what data to present, what examples to share, and when to share them. You'll also discover the power of competition and effective ways to capture audience attention through the introduction.

EXERCISE: ELEVATOR PITCH

With your 4-point formula, you're ready to craft an elevator pitch. Follow the process below to produce your elevator pitch:

PROBLEM → SOLUTION → BENEFITS
(OPTIONAL: → MARKET)

1. Describe the PROBLEM you're addressing in one sentence
2. Share your SOLUTION by delivering your one-sentence UVP
3. Briefly list the BENEFITS of your solution in one sentence
4. (optional: share a competitor and explain your competitive advantage)

Example:
Gardens die all the time because people over or under-water their plants. PlantGarder is an iPhone app that reminds people when to water their plants. With our reminders, you minimize water use and keep your plants looking beautiful. (And compared to PlantTimer, we're a more affordable solution with a cleaner interface that makes it easy for anyone to use.)

CHAPTER SUMMARY

1. Effective pitches are ordered Problem-Solution-Market-Business
2. Focus on a simple problem description, the problem pains, and opportunity trends
3. Craft your solution with a UVP, demo, and product benefits
4. Ensure you target your market accurately, measure the size, and show you can seize it
5. Explain how you capture the market with your go-to-market and revenue strategies

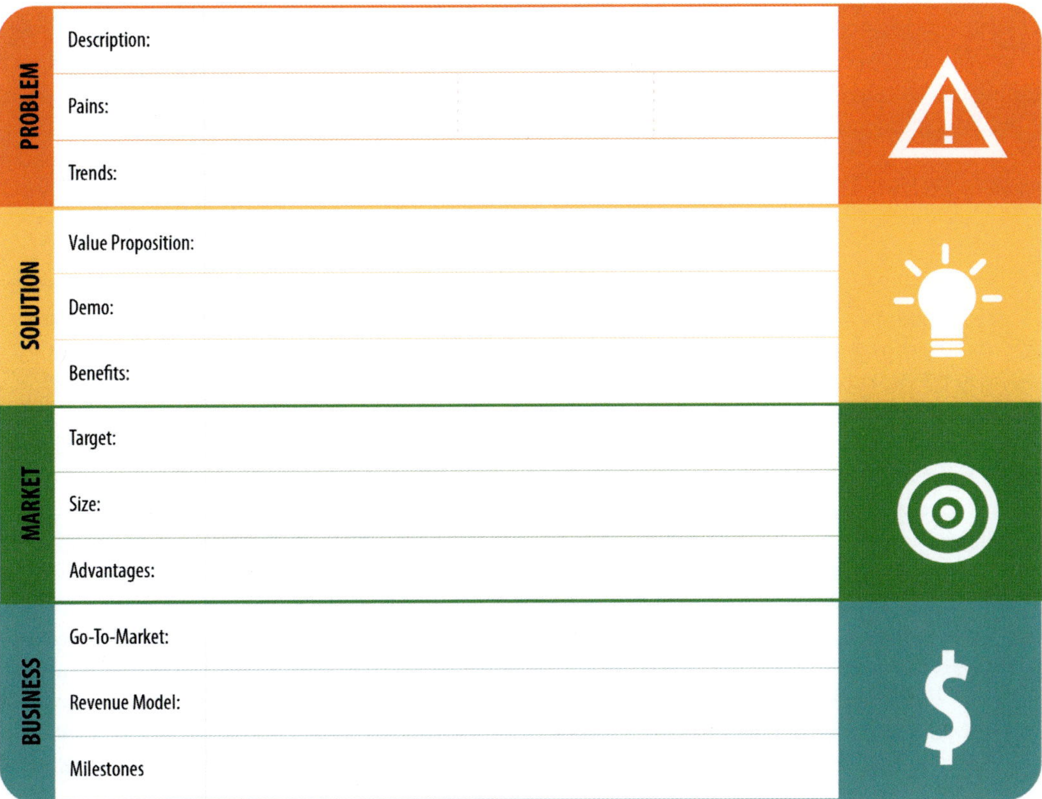

Download at **pitchpower.org**

Enigma

2013 TechCrunch Disrupt Winning Pitch

Hello, good afternoon. My name is Marc DaCosta, co-founder of Enigma. Enigma is a search and discovery platform for public data. But what do I mean when I talk about public data?

Think about an event like South-by-Southwest. South-by-Southwest has ripples in hundreds of public databases. There are containers of swag coming in from China and showing up in US customs databases. There are a lot of high profile attendees, some of whom are coming in from private planes, showing up in flight plans databases. At night, tens of thousands of people are crowding the bars, causing a spike in Texas alcohol sales tax receipt databases. And the list goes on. This kind of public data is valuable because it's a reflection of the real world and it reveals things that you won't find by looking at Twitter hash tags or Foursquare check-ins, but there's a problem here.

← Enigma works in an uncommon space, so they provide context to help the audience understand that space

While this data is public, and while it is out there, it's not really accessible. Today, public data comes in all kinds of different shapes and forms. Everything from restrictive web portals, to messy FTP sites to 1970's database formats and everything else in between. Doing something as simple as a search across all of this public data is not even possible. And what that means is, upfront, you're limited by the sources of data that you know about. And what's more, because this data is locked away in silos, it's impossible to see the relationships and the connections between these sources of public data. What public data needs is an infrastructure, and that's what we're building at Enigma.

← Here begins a description of the Problem followed by Problem pains.

At Enigma, we're building a scalable infrastructure for acquiring, indexing and searching public data. And now, my co-founder Hicham will show you what that looks like.

← Enigma transitions into its Solution with the UVP

Hey there, my name is Hicham Oudghiri, let's switch over to the live demo. Ok, why don't we search something like Google for instance in Enigma, alright now what you're seeing are all of the results for Google in Enigma. I mean, we're indexing over a 100 thousand data sets, billions of records and Google is showing up in you know, government filings, property records, even immigration, right.

← The demo immediately follows the UVP.

So it's interesting, because there's been a lot of debate about that topic, about skilled work and immigration in tech. Let's check out this H-1B Visa data set. It's put up by the department of labor. Alright, now we have every single H-1B applications in 2012, filtered to Google. We can ask questions of these data sets, so let's click on the salary column. Alright, we learn that Google is actually spending 87 million dollars tracking foreign labor. Why don't we do something deeper like actually distribute all of this data across the job titles that these people are being hired for. Ok, so now we see Google's allocating 60 million towards software engineers, and so it's only when we scroll all the way down that we see that they're only spending 467 thousand dollars on designers.

Now, it's not a lot and it's interesting, but it's even more interesting when we compare these things. So why don't we filter this data set to Facebook. Great, so now we have Facebook's visa applications up. Let's see how much they're spending total. 20 million dollars. Now that's 3 times less than Google. In fact, if you actually

← Enigma demos a second use-case

look on the left, they're spending more on designers. That could explain why my profile page keeps changing every three months, but you get the idea.

List of benefits →

What we do at Enigma is that we really let you find and manipulate the data that you're looking for. Let's jump back to the search results; I want to show you that Enigma is also about discovering new data sets you didn't even know existed or are relevant. So you're looking at these results, and you see how you can build a rich portrait of a company like Google. Check out FCC licenses, maybe latest registrations for Google Glass are in there. Lobbying records, you now see what kind of issues Google is really getting behind and putting money towards. Private investments or even map out all of Google's subsidiaries.

Enigma demos a 3rd-use case →

Now here's something that caught our eye at Enigma, Google popping out in a Department of Energy data set. Let's go check it out, and look at what the DOE has on Google. So now what you're looking at is the data set of every single electricity contract purchase in the United States. And we learned, that Google is actually operating as a utility, buying electricity directly for itself. Let's see who it's buying electricity from.

Ok, a lot of wind companies; and it's interesting because we know that Google has been pushing for sustainability in its operations. But now we actually see that play out in data. We see with Enigma, you can break down to how many Megawatts are being distributed to which facilities, how long these contracts are hedged out for, and so on.

I want to take a break, I want to show you how you can get to this sort of insight without even being on the web app. So what if I just browsing on the internet, going to the Google energy investments webpage. With our browser plugin, it's on the right. Let's go and enable it, all of the entities on the page light up. So companies, people, locations, and I can do something like click on clean power finance, be routed back to that level of granularity, see maybe government grants for that specific contract in Enigma.

Enigma touches upon go-to market →

We're excited today, what we want to switch back to the presentation for a second, because we have a lot to announce. A lot of people have been pioneering how we analyze the world with data, but what we're disrupting here is something much more fundamental, you know, issues of infrastructure and content. And we're launching our web app API with partners who really share this vision. So the Gerson Lehman Group in Finance, the New York Times in news media who've just come on board as strategic investor, S&P Capital IQ and the Harvard Business School.

Ends with their vision →

Every day, without the pain of working with data and acquiring it, they're showing us how they're leveraging it in their work and in their thinking. And that's what excites us the most, really exposing this world that just been hidden for way too long. And that going forward, we'll make us think about, how we define the structured web and the limits of public knowledge in general.

Thank you.

CHAPTER 3

ELEMENTS OF INFLUENCE

To win funding, you need more than a formula. You're not aiming to be one of the best pitches an investor sees all week, but the best they see all year.

3. ELEMENTS OF INFLUENCE

Problem
Solution
Market
Business
Tailoring influence
Stormpulse's pitch

Chapter 3 Elements of Influence

To win funding, you need more than a formula. A formula is the foundation for a strong pitch; but it's not enough. You're not aiming to be one of the best pitches an investor sees all week; you're aiming to be one of the best they see all year.

TO BE THE BEST, YOU MUST PROVE WHAT YOU PITCH IS TRUE.

It's not enough to simply describe the problem and share your solution, market, and business. You need to prove there's a problem, prove your solution solves the problem, prove there's a market, and prove the efficacy of your business model.

When Enigma won the $50,000 grand prize in 2013 for their stellar problem-solution pitch, they used persuasion to prove to the audience they were a startup worth reckoning with. You can pitch as well as or better than Enigma to win the investment you need for success. Last chapter gave you the outline; now you're ready to present your pitch in a powerful and persuasive manner.

Persuasion follows the "Anna Karenina principle." As Tolstoy famously wrote at the start of that novel, "Happy families are all alike; every unhappy family is unhappy in its own way." Likewise, there are numerous ways a pitch can fail to be persuasive; but a persuasive pitch always comes down to the same axiom: an irrefutable quartet of elements that – if used judiciously -- fulfills the happy formula for success.

In 2001, Harvard Business Review published an exemplary paper on persuasion resulting from four years of field research amongst business leaders. Author Jay Conger concluded that persuasive proposals have four main elements: credibility, audience value, data, and emotional connection. These elements are similar to those outlined in the popular marketing book Made to Stick. The advice dates back even to the days of the Greek philosopher Aristotle, who claimed that persuasion required ethos (credibility), pathos (emotion), and logos (logic/facts).

Based on research and verified by successful pitches, THE KEY INGREDIENTS OF PERSUASION ARE: CREDIBILITY, AUDIENCE VALUE, DATA, AND STORY. Credibility is your perceived knowledge and expertise regarding the topic of discussion. Doctors have significant credibility when discussing all things medical. Audience value means tailoring your message to fit potential benefits to the listeners. Investors want to hear how your startup provides low risk high return.

DATA ARE THE FACTS, THE RESEARCH, THE STATISTICS. WHAT'S THE EVIDENCE THAT YOUR SOLUTION OR BUSINESS PLAN WORKS? STORY IS THE EMOTIONAL COMPONENT, THE CUSTOMER ANECDOTES, YOUR OWN EXPERIENCE. DATA IS NEITHER MEANINGFUL NOR MEMORABLE WITHOUT TOUCHING THE EMOTIONS, SO PLUG INTO THE VAST FIELD OF HUMAN EXPERIENCE.

In this book, these ingredients are referred to as **Elements of Influence**. The Elements of Influence apply to each of the four points in your pitch. Last chapter you learned that successful pitches follow the formula of Problem-Solution-Market-Business. When you add Elements of Influence, you independently apply these elements to each of the four points. In other words, you apply credibility, audience value, data, and story to the problem. Later, you apply different credibility, audience value, data, and story to the solution. Notice for example, if you display data about the problem, it does nothing to convince investors that you have a working solution or a viable market opportunity. You need to apply different data to the solution and likewise the market and business. Each point of your pitch is proven independent of the others, and it's your job to apply Elements of Influence independently to the points that matter most.

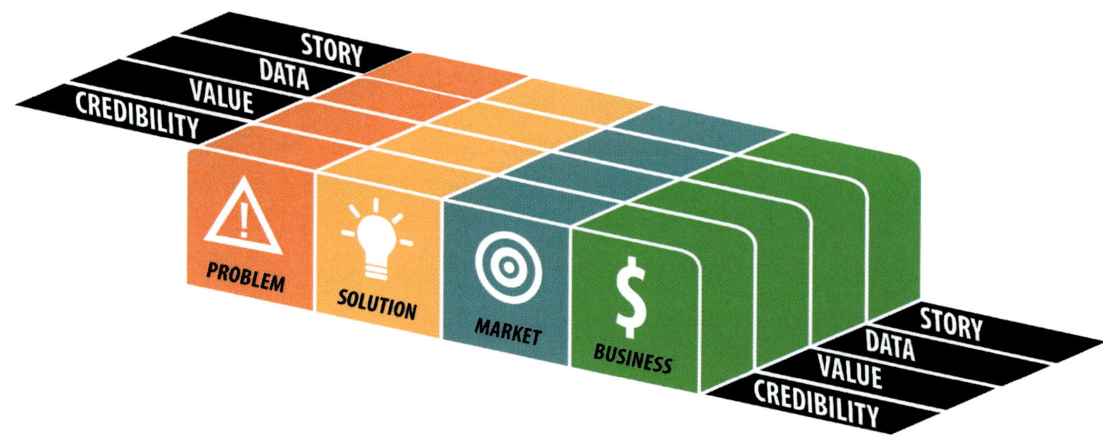

Unlike the 4-Point Pitch which flows in a linear progression, the Elements of Influence can be applied in any order to individual points.

CONSIDER THE ELEMENTS AS INGREDIENTS TO BAKING THE ULTIMATE BATCH OF POINTS. YOU NEED TO ADD ALL THE INGREDIENTS SO AUDIENCES SWALLOW ANY POINT IN YOUR PITCH, BUT YOU CAN MIX THOSE INGREDIENTS TOGETHER IN DIFFERENT WAYS. MIX THESE INGREDIENTS TOGETHER IN WHATEVER WAY WORKS FOR YOU TO PRODUCE THE MOST FLAVORFUL OUTCOME.

This chapter helps you determine how to identify the different elements for each of the 4 points, empowering you to deliver persuasively what investors need to know in order to invest in you.

Problem

In 2012, **Kindara** CEO Kati Bicknell pitched her women's fertility app at Founder Showcase. Unfortunately, more than half her audience were unmarried men unfamiliar with the challenges of female fertility. Could she prove to this audience there really was problem? She began by sharing her mother's struggles to conceive children; she then introduced data to show the number of other women facing similar hurdles. Bicknell used the Elements of Influence to prove the problem. As a result, she tied for first place for best pitch at the event.

When you face an audience unfamiliar with the problem you're solving or that doesn't grasp the magnitude of the issue, you must take steps as Bicknell did to prove the problem. Effective proof (i.e., persuasion) requires you add the elements of credibility, audience value, data, and story.

Credibility

Credibility is your perceived knowledge or expertise about the problem. The most effective way to establish credibility is to explain your problem in a clear and concise manner. The more clearly you explain the problem, the more you sound as though you know what you're talking about. The more you sound like you know what you're talking about, the more investors assume you know what you're talking about. Conversely, if you stumble through your problem description, investors assume you don't know what you're talking about. When Bicknell pitched Kindara, she explained the problem in a straight-forward way that everyone in the audience, male or female, could understand.

A SECOND WAY TO SHOW CREDIBILITY IS TO CONNECT YOURSELF TO THE PROBLEM EITHER DIRECTLY OR INDIRECTLY. If you or someone you know suffers from the problem, share that fact. Likewise, if you've had exposure to the problem space through your previous work, share that exposure.

Bicknell's pitch shared the struggles of her mother, making her pitch personal. Bicknell's relationship with her mother's struggles, including the fact that Bicknell herself is female, gave her a strong connection to the problem space of female fertility and thus reinforced her credibility. I was in the audience that day to witness Bicknell's delivery, and she convinced me she knew the problem space well. No wonder she tied for first place.

A final way to establish credibility is to borrow the credibility of experts by sharing expert opinions of the problem.[1] When post-doc Oren Knopfmacher, a member of the Stanford Leaders in Communication organization I co-founded, pitched his medical sensor device to investors over the telephone (an especially difficult medium), he had a director from Stanford Hospital on the line to confirm the problem was real. When the director spoke, his opinion created a palpable response in investors. In effect, Knopfmacher borrowed the credibility of the hospital director to persuade investors there was a problem.

Overall, there are several ways to establish credibility. Share your problem clearly, relate yourself to the problem, or borrow the credibility of experts. Of these three, the first is the most powerful. Make it clear!

1 *Robert Cialdini, Influence: The Psychology of Persuasion (HarperBusiness, 2006).*

Audience Value

Adding audience value to your problem is like adding sugar to the cookie mix. It sweetens the deal. Investors are interested in low risk high return, and you want to show the problem creates just such an opportunity. To establish low risk high return, demonstrate that the problem has significant negative impact. The worse the problem, the more you convince investors there is demand for your solution. Make it interesting.

ONE WAY TO SHOW NEGATIVE IMPACT IS TO INDICATE THE TOTAL NUMBER OF PEOPLE SUFFERING FROM THE PROBLEM. The more people suffering from the problem, the larger the potential market for a solution. This signifies high return. During Kindara's pitch, Bicknell said that "many women" still share the experiences of her mother. When you pitch, you can be even more specific by offering statistics that demonstrate exactly how many people suffer. These numbers obviously do not represent your target market, but they give investors a glimpse into the magnitude of the problem and send the message that this is a lucrative opportunity.

Another way to show negative impact is by highlighting the magnitude of problem pains, including inefficiency, inaccessibility, and dollars. The greater the pain, the more likely people will seek a solution. During Kindara's pitch, Bicknell explained that women today spend $500 million on fertility kits at home and $4 billion on reproductive treatments. Why? Because fertility directly affects the fundamental ability to have a family. It took Bicknell only 15 seconds to communicate the full impact of such pain to both women and men. Short and crisp.

When you pitch, share the size of the problem and magnitude of problem pains to sweeten things up and gain investor attention. Audience value captures interest. Make it interesting!

Data

The final two Elements of Influence are data and story. These form the foundation to your pitch. Data make the problem real. Data show the problem isn't just an entrepreneur's opinion. Without cold hard facts to support what you're saying, you can't prove anything. Examples of data include statistics, character cases, and quotes.[2]

When you pitch the size of the problem and the magnitude of the problem pains, use statistics and character cases to prove what you say is true. Bicknell used the case of her mother as well as data on the amount of money women spend annually on fertility treatments to show the problem Kindara addressed.

To emphasize the need, share quotes. For example, you can quote the complaints of people with the problem. Humans are programmed to value the opinions of others, and investors are more likely to agree there's a problem if they hear quotes from people with the problem.[3]

Be prudent when sharing data. Present data only when relevant; don't share data simply for the sake of sharing it. Data alone is meaningless; it must be used to illustrate your point. The purpose of presenting data during the problem is to provide proof of the size, magnitude of pains, and need related to the problem.

When you present data, either through statistics, cases, or quotes, you ground the problem in reality. To be convincing, reality is where you need to stand. Make it real!

2 *In Startup Garage, an influential course taught at Stanford Graduate School of Business, Russell Siegelman, partner emeritus at Kleiner Perkins, lectures on the importance of data and research.*

3 *Noah Goldstein, Steve Martin, & Robert Cialdini, Yes! 50 Scientifically Proven Ways to Be Persuasive (Free Press, 2008).*

Story

IT'S NOT ENOUGH TO SIMPLY MAKE THE PROBLEM REAL, YOU ALSO NEED TO BRING THE PROBLEM TO LIFE. RESEARCH SUGGESTS THAT EMOTIONS UNDERPIN DECISION MAKING.[4]

Emotions also motivate action. If you want investors to invest in you, share stories that convey emotion. Arouse your audience's empathy.

The best stories to share are those of people suffering with the problem. When Bicknell pitched at Founder Showcase, the highlight of her pitch was the story of her mother. Bicknell shared her mother's experience with infertility by saying "these were the worst years of her life" when she felt "alone and confused." Bicknell expressed the emotions of her mother's suffering through her voice, emphasizing the pain in her tone. The feelings she inspired in the room were palpable, and I could hear people catching their breath as she spoke.

By sharing her mother's story, Bicknell made a lasting impression on the audience. According to research, people recall data only 5 percent of the time after hearing them, whereas people recall stories a whopping 63 percent of the time.[5] The story clearly stuck with me when I chose pitch examples to include in this book. If you want your words to stick in the minds of investors, share a story.

Other examples of story include anecdotes, analogies, and metaphors that convey the person's experience, particularly the pain. In the words of Nancy Duarte, founder of Duarte Design – the world's largest presentations firm for businesses – "if two products have the same features, the one that appeals to an emotional need will be chosen." Remember that when you step in front of investors, your competition for funding is the hundreds of other startups that walk through their door. Every advantage counts.

Stories remain equally important even when pitching business-to-business (B2B) products. If you're pitching a B2B product, you may not have the freedom to go into the same depth of personal experience that Bicknell did with her mother. However, stories help build a context of understanding around people with the problem, the pain, and the business results if that pain continues. The experiences we feel at work are very different from those in our personal lives, but these experiences are equally valid to making your pitch memorable.

Data and story are often presented together, with data supporting the story. For example, if you present the story of someone suffering with the problem, you create an emotional context which investors can relate to. If you then present data that show 2 million others are also suffering, you've used data to amplify the initial emotions. Contrast this with presenting the data first and then the story. In such a case, the data makes the problem real but does not enhance the impact of the story. Figure out what ways you can combine data and story to generate the most impact in investors.

When you share stories, introduce someone suffering from the problem. When you do, you create meaning. Make it meaningful!

---

4 *In particular, note research by Antonio Damasio: http://en.wikipedia.org/wiki/Somatic_marker_hypothesis*

5 *Chip Heath and Dan Heath, Made to Stick: Why Some Ideas Survive and Others Die, (New York: Random House, 2007).*

An Influential Problem

To prove the problem, inject the elements of credibility, audience value, data, and story into your pitch. MAKE IT CLEAR. MAKE IT INTERESTING. MAKE IT REAL. MAKE IT MEANINGFUL. WHEN YOU DO, YOU WIN.

When Exactuals' CEO Mike Hurst pitched his payment system for Hollywood actors that you read about in the last chapter, he had to prove the unfamiliar problem associated with residuals payments in the Hollywood industry. The pitch started with a video of an actor ranting about how ridiculous the existing payment system was – data and story. Hurst then introduced how he discovered the problem while working with the Screen Actors Guild – credibility. He continued his pitch by explaining the current process the studios, payroll houses, and guilds went through to write and deliver paper checks to thousands of actors each week – data. Hurst also shared that if you walked into the room where the checks are processed today, you would find a very hectic scene with banker's boxes full of paper being moved back and forth – story again. Hurst showed that current payment methods cost the industry as much as $5 per check and many payments were delayed by months due to errors and inefficiency – audience value.

Overall, Hurst proved the problem with the Elements of Influence. Using this pitch, he launched himself into orbit with an oversubscribed seed round of $900,000. More recently, Hurst successfully closed his Series A. When you take steps to prove your problem, you take steps that will launch you into orbit as well.

SECTION SUMMARY

Credibility

• Your perceived knowledge and expertise around the problem
• Explain the problem clearly
• Relate yourself to the problem directly or indirectly
• Share expert opinions about the problem

Audience Value

• How the problem presents opportunity for low risk high return
• Share the number of people suffering from the problem
• Describe the magnitude of the problem pains

Data

• Proof that the problem is real
• Provide data on the size and magnitude of the problem
• Use individual cases and quotes to highlight the need

Story

• Human experience that brings the problem to life
• Share the story of someone with the problem
• Use anecdotes, analogies, and metaphors that illustrate the experience of the problem

EXERCISE: PROVE THE PROBLEM

1. Create a story of a person or business (real or hypothetical) with the problem. Fill in any necessary background details to make the story clear.

2. Emphasize problem pains the person or company in your story experiences. Add data to reinforce either the magnitude of the pain or the total number of people/ companies suffering from the pain.

3. Relate yourself to the story if you can – how are you personally aware of this problem?

Remember to keep the length relative to the knowledge investors already have about the problem. The more they know, the less description you need to give them.

After you complete the exercises above, you have a better feel for how to craft an engaging and influential problem scenario. In essence, you're ramping up your pitch from a bland-vanilla message into a meaningful and memorable taste of opportunity.

Solution

After you convince your audience there's a problem, you must prove your solution solves the problem. Last chapter you read how ZocDoc demoed their way to over $90 million. If you were to go online and watch ZocDoc's 2007 pitch, you'd see they used the Elements of Influence in their solution to capture investor attention.

Credibility

Make it clear. SIMPLICITY IS THE MOST IMPORTANT PERSUASIVE TECHNIQUE TO GARNER CREDIBILITY, AND THAT'S WHY YOUR SINGLE-SENTENCE UVP CARRIES THE MOST WEIGHT IN THE PRESENTATION OF YOUR SOLUTION. When ZocDoc pitched at TechCrunch Disrupt, they established credibility by having a simple explanation of the product. First, they delivered a clear UVP: "ZocDoc is an online way to book doctor and dentist appointments instantly." The founders then gave a concise description of ZocDoc's ease and use.

The second way to establish credibility is to share your background in the solution space. Think for a moment, ARE YOU THE RIGHT PERSON TO SOLVE THE PROBLEM? Of course you are, so explain why! If you've worked in the current industry or launched a product before, don't hesitate to tell investors.

When you share your relevant skills or experience, you increase the chance that investors will listen to your words favorably. While ZocDoc demoed their product, COO and founder Oliver Kharraz briefly mentioned that he was a physician. By sharing his background, Kharraz could then speak credibly about physician care and why doctors would use their service.

You can also share your activity in developing the current solution. If you've pivoted, tell investors. Pivots show experience in identifying product-market fit. When you highlight your involvement in product development and lessons learned, you show yourself to be a better investment than someone who hasn't explored whether they developed a good solution.

Your goal is to improve the impact of your words by convincing investors you know what you're talking about, so share just enough of your background to bring attention to your words. This isn't necessarily about your team. In my experience, investors don't need a lot of details about the team until they're excited about the startup; that's one reason why teams are often presented at the end of a pitch. Rather, share what makes you the right person to create your solution.

Not everyone has a background relevant to the solution space, and that's ok. Expert opinions such as quotes and journal articles have been used to substitute for credibility. Just as Knopfmacher had a director at Stanford Hospital to confirm the problem, YOU CAN CAPTURE THE OPINION OF AN EXPERT TO VALIDATE YOUR SOLUTION TO THAT PROBLEM.

The risk of not establishing credibility is that if investors compare you to 10 other entrepreneurs with similar products, who will they choose? There are many factors, but one factor will likely be whether you're the right person to solve the problem.

Overall, to establish credibility around your solution, describe your product clearly, share your relevant background and experience, and share your work towards the current solution. Remember that the heart of credibility rests in your ability to concisely deliver your product explanation. If you sound like you know what you're talking about, people assume you know what you're talking about. Conversely, if you have trouble explaining exactly what your solution offers, you are unlikely to inspire much confidence. Make it clear!

Audience Value

Time to make it interesting. As we saw in the previous chapter, part of introducing the solution is to sell benefits over product features. BENEFITS CREATE VALUE. ZocDoc explained how collecting patient feedback about physicians (feature) helps users choose the right doctor for their malady (benefit). This was the correct approach for a TechCrunch audience composed primarily of potential customers. ZocDoc could have gone a step further if they were pitching to investors.

INVESTORS ARE INTERESTED IN LOW RISK HIGH RETURN, AND YOU CAN STRENGTHEN YOUR PITCH BY TRANSLATING CUSTOMER BENEFITS INTO INVESTOR BENEFITS. Translating customer benefits into investor benefits requires adding a step to the features-benefits conversion. If ZocDoc were pitching exclusively to investors, they could have delivered their pitch as follows: ZocDoc collects patient feedback about physicians (feature), which helps users choose the right doctor (customer benefit). When customers meet with the right doctors, they experience higher satisfaction and are more likely to recommend ZocDoc to their friends (investor benefit). Bingo! By translating a customer benefit into an investor benefit, ZocDoc could show that their feature would lead to higher potential return.

Let's look at one more example. When Steve Jobs introduced the iPod in 2001, he said it had 20-minute skip protection (feature), so you never miss a beat when exercising (customer benefit). If Steve Jobs were pitching the iPod to investors, he might have taken an additional step and said: Because people can use the iPod when exercising, we have greater consumer reach (investor benefit).

Think about the customer benefits your product offers.

HOW DO THESE BENEFITS PROMOTE MARKET OR BUSINESS ADVANTAGES THAT INVESTORS CARE ABOUT?

Quicker, faster, cheaper are all benefits to customers. If you take the extra step to translate these customer benefits into investor benefits, you gain influence. Make it interesting!

Data

Make it real. To present data on the viability of your solution, show your product. There is no substitute for a good demo, and ZocDoc proved it with a great pitch in 2007. Last chapter outlined how to present an effective demo.

Additional data can also be used to complement your demo. Share the resources you gathered to build the solution, the research you performed to evolve the product, and how you responded to user feedback. For example, ZocDoc shared that they had done "extensive user testing" to ensure a simple user interface. Successful solutions are rarely created in vacuums; instead, they are developed and tested both in-house and by users in the field. Share this testing. You can even present case studies or quotes of people using the product to show product-customer fit. Make it real!

Story

MAKE IT MEANINGFUL.
WRAP EMOTIONAL CONTEXT AROUND YOUR SOLUTION.

One way to create meaning is to ensure your demo is relatable. When ZocDoc pitched their demo, founder Karraz walked through the product as a hypothetical customer who had just broken his tooth. First, Karraz sought out a local dentist using the web service. He showed how easy it was to locate a good dentist and schedule an appointment online. The audience experienced the product from a customer perspective during this hypothetical emergency, allowing them to understand the value of ZocDoc's simplicity and convenience when it mattered.

When choosing which story to share during your demo, you can relate back to the story introduced in the problem. If you introduced the story of a suffering person in the problem, explain how your solution now addresses that same person's pains and brings freedom and benefits to their life. Relating back to the problem story creates continuity between the problem and solution and is particularly effective for B2B solutions.

You can also share stories from user engagements. For example, if while testing the product you met a user who suggested a brilliant new feature, share the story. By doing so, you bring to life your product development.

Stories bring emotional experience to the product. The most common and perhaps most effective storytelling device is demoing your product from the perspective of a real or hypothetical person with the problem. In doing so, you show how your product has a meaningful impact on the user. Make it meaningful!

SECTION SUMMARY

Credibility

- Provide a clear and concise product description via your UVP
- Highlight any relevant background experience in developing solutions
- Share what you've learned while developing the current product

Audience Value

- Translate customer benefits into investor benefits

Data

- Demo your product
- Share product tests and customer feedback

Story

- Demo your product from the perspective of someone with the problem
- Share user-engagement stories

EXERCISE: SUPPORT YOUR SOLUTION

1. In one sentence, explain why you're the right person(s) to create this solution. How does this work tie in with your background? Avoid going into detail.

2. Revisit the list of benefits you created in Chapter 2 and translate customer benefits into investor benefits.

3. Revisit the demo exercise from Chapter 2 and confirm whether it emphasizes the emotions necessary for the story to be meaningful .

These exercises are geared to add credibility and emotion to your solution. When you integrate the exercises above into the solution exercises from last chapter, you create a harmony between the solution flow and the Elements of Influence.

Market

A GREAT SOLUTION BEGS A MARKET, BUT IS THERE REALLY A MARKET?

Investors probe to find out, and you want to prove there is indeed opportunity. When successful startup DoorDash pitched their online food-delivery service to investors, they used the Elements of Influence to present the market persuasively. Their skills met with success. Here's how you can meet with success too.

Credibility

Make it clear. When you have a clear target market, you establish credibility. The more clearly you identify your market, the more credibility you win.

KNOWLEDGE IS ALSO CREDIBILITY. When you demonstrate your knowledge of the market landscape and trends, you convince investors that you understand the market you're entering. When Evan Moore and his co-founders won the chance to pitch DoorDash to incubator Y Combinator, this was their big chance. Wired Magazine calls Y Combinator "the tech world's most prestigious program for budding digital entrepreneurs," but going through Y Combinator's pitch process can feel like going through a grinder. The investors hammered Moore repeatedly with tough questions during his pitch. Moore had answers. By studying the market, competition, and involving himself hands-on with customers, he talked fluently about market landscape and how the market evolved. Through his answers, he persuaded Y Combinator to accept DoorDash into the program.

Part of knowing the market landscape is awareness to your competition: WHO'S OUT THERE AND WHAT'S THEIR MARKET SHARE/DIFFERENTIATION. You'd be hard-pressed if you weren't prepared with this information. Almost everybody has a competitor, even when it's not obvious. Sometimes competition comes through an alternative solution, other times it comes from companies who could enter the market in the future. For example, when Taiwan opened a high speed railway in 2007 connecting cities in the north and south halves of the country, the railway had almost no competition from other railways; however, airlines ferried passengers in the sky between north and south. This alternative essentially competed for customers looking to travel.

When introducing competitors, you can further demonstrate your market knowledge by understanding the costs customers incur when switching from your competition to you. To continue the example above, if airlines in Taiwan have loyalty programs like frequent fliers' clubs, customers would be more locked in and less likely to switch to the new railway. This is the switching cost, and it helps describe the market landscape.

Trends can impact markets. If you talk fluently on social, economic, technology, or political trends that affect your market, you show knowledge that supports credibility. For example, in California the government frequently passes legislation promoting less pollution (political trend). Similarly, California consumers like myself are increasingly making decisions that protect the environment (social trend). If you're developing a clean-air technology for consumers in California, you can reference both political and social trends like these to support a competitive advantage in the target market.

Finally, when I interviewed Clint Korver, a co-founder and partner at Ulu Ventures, he said he looks for market-team coherence. Is there something special about you or your team that gives you an advantage in the marketplace? For example, if you created a new hotel service and your father happened to be good friends with the president of Hilton Hotels & Resorts, you have unique connections and access to knowledge that others with a similar service lack.

Overall there are many ways to analyze the market and competition. Above are some ideas, but this book is about pitching and not market analysis. For more detailed examples, reference other resources such as Michael Porter's "Five Forces."

WHILE KNOWLEDGE IS PART OF CREDIBILITY, REMEMBER THAT ULTIMATELY CONCISION IS MORE IMPORTANT THAN CONTENT. Knowing your market helps you present perspective and answer questions; but don't share market information in your pitch unless it's necessary to explain your target, size, or competitive advantages. Make it clear!

Audience Value

MAKE IT INTERESTING TO INVESTORS BY APPEALING TO LOW RISK HIGH RETURN. When you follow the formula from last chapter, you show low risk through your ability to seize the market and high return by measuring the market size.

You can lower risk further by introducing barriers to entry. Barriers to entry are obstacles that make it difficult for competitors to enter the same market. Barriers include special access to limited resources, intellectual property such as patents, and special agreements with partners or governments.

Elon Musk, co-founder of PayPal and Tesla Motors, founded SpaceX in 2002 to take humanity a step closer to being a spacefaring civilization. During an interview at TED, Musk implied that economic barriers with space travel are so astronomical that even governments have trouble developing cost-efficient ships without the right technology (which he was developing).

TO HIGHLIGHT HIGH RETURN, APPEAL TO MARKET SIZE AND SCALE; BUT BE WARNED THAT WHAT YOU SHOW CAN ADVERSELY IMPACT YOUR PITCH. IF YOUR SIZE IS NOT REALISTIC, IT CAN BACKLASH ON YOUR CREDIBILITY. Mark Cuban, Chairman of AXS.tv and owner of the Dallas Mavericks professional basketball team, sits on the panel of investors for the popular pitch show Shark Tank. In 2012 Cuban was pitched the company Liquid Money, a cologne that smells like cash. The pitch was engaging, but Cuban said he would not invest because the entrepreneur made a "cardinal mistake." According to Cuban, whenever an entrepreneur says the market is huge and they only need to capture a small percent of the market to be successful, his red flag goes up.

IF YOUR FOCUS IS MORE ABOUT NUMBERS AND LESS ABOUT SPECIFIC CUSTOMERS, YOU MAY LOSE CREDIBILITY IN THE EYES OF INVESTORS. Assumptions of the market as a single vast group of people may be viewed as an overgeneralization, suggesting you don't know your market well enough to focus on where you'll be effective. In the case of Liquid Money, one must wonder what a customer looks like who fits into a "small percent." By targeting a percent of some larger market, you fail to see the individual market segments and unique customers that can be realistically addressed. You're looking at clouds, not customers. There's no benefit there.

Target and measure your market accurately to ensure investors resonate with the size. Once they resonate with an accurate size, they begin to see high return. Make it interesting!

Data

Make it real. TO PROVE YOUR MARKET IS REAL, PROVIDE EVIDENCE OF MARKET INTEREST AND MARKET SIZE. The clearest way to show market interest and size is to share the volume and tenor of interactions you've had with potential customers. Before Evan Moore and his co-founders pitched DoorDash to Y Combinator, they went out and tested the market first-hand. With a delivery service on the road, they shared the number of phone calls they received and the number of restaurants that had expressed interest in working with them. Not all the talks led to business, but that was irrelevant. What mattered was the number of interested potential customers.

WHEN POTENTIAL CUSTOMERS EXPRESS INTEREST IN YOUR PRODUCT, THIS OFFERS EVIDENCE OF CONCRETE MARKET DEMAND. People who reach out obviously need something, and your goal is to prove a market exists. Some entrepreneurs misunderstand customer interest and are afraid to discuss customers who didn't wind up purchasing their product. The truth is, there are many reasons customers may not go with your solution – maybe they don't have a budget yet, maybe they're not first-movers, maybe they're still making plans. Whatever the case, the number of customers who reach out to you, regardless if they purchase your product or not, evidences market need. If there's a market, investors may get excited because slight modifications to your product or business plan could ignite a deluge of sales.

You don't have to wait for customers to reach out to you; you can also reach out to them. If you want to validate your market, make calls to a few dozen prospective customers and gauge their interest in discussing the product more. Share the results with investors. In the words of popular author and serial entrepreneur Steve Blank, "get out of the building."

Another powerful and often misunderstood way to prove your market is through competition. Angel investor and Stanford Lecturer Steve Ciesinski instructs students and business professionals to use competition to validate the market. If there's a competitor, there must be a market supporting the competitor's business. Brilliant proof![6]

Recall the elevator pitch from last chapter. When you include a sentence about the market in your elevator pitch, you show credibility by knowing the competition, audience value through competitive advantage, and data by using the competition to confirm an existing market. Everything fits together.

A final way to prove your market is to share third-party data that validate assumptions of market size. One entrepreneur I coached used survey data to show the percent of the addressable market segment that wanted his service. These data evidenced real need.

When you discuss the market, think about the data you have on your market. How many people have you talked to, what competition is out there, do you have available market data. Markets are ideas, and numbers make them real!

6 *When discussing competition, be brief. Recall from Chapter 2 that the more time you spend discussing a topic, the more important it may appear.*

Story

Make it meaningful. To make your data meaningful with story, provide examples of enthusiastic responses from potential customers. If you've made phone calls or met with potential customers, you might recall particular anecdotes when certain customers responded eagerly. Share them. These stories give you the opportunity to share the customer's enthusiasm, and they may also give you the chance to expand on what made them so excited. For example, perhaps when you met with a potential customer and shared a certain feature differentiating you from the competition, the potential customer showed positive surprise and arranged a follow-up meeting. A story like this would make your product sound great.

When the founders of DoorDash presented their first-hand evidence of market demand, they did it through sharing field stories. They talked about some of the phone calls they had received, including the discussions and experiences they encountered while working with potential customers. The stories involved both customers and themselves. Through these descriptions, investors experienced the feeling that there really was a market. Make it meaningful!

SECTION SUMMARY

Credibility

• Have a clear target market

• Be sure you understand the market landscape, including competition and market trends

Audience Value

• Lower risk by showing you can seize the market and mentioning barriers to entry

• Heighten return by accurately measuring your market size and path to sustainability

Data

• Highlight the volume of your interaction with potential customers

• Introduce competitors that are already successful in your market

• Present 3rd party research on the size of your market

Story

• Share engagement stories with (potential) customers

EXERCISE: MEASURE YOUR MARKET

1. Identify at least one trend or barrier to entry that gives you an edge in your market.

2. Acquire data on the size of your target market.

3. Share a story of your engagement with a potential customer, emphasizing the customer's positive reaction to your product or their need to find a solution.

You now have content to show greater advantage in the market, support your market size assumptions, and bring to life your potential customers. Great job completing this exercise set!

Business

Every investor wants to know whether you can leverage the market opportunity. Naturally, you must prove you can. Successful startup RidePal used the Elements of Influence to present their business plan persuasively and win funding. You can use these elements to help show you've got a real business too.

Credibility

Make it clear. To establish credibility, you must deliver a clear and logical business plan.

REMEMBER THAT INVESTORS INVEST IN YOU. INVESTORS DON'T JUST ANALYZE THE NUMBERS, THEY ANALYZE YOUR LOGIC TO SEE HOW YOU THINK.

In many startups, the data around the business rest on untested assumptions. Successful VC Peter Thiel says that even though the business plan is mostly a fiction for young companies, you should be able to talk about it. Can you talk fluently about your go-to-market strategy and revenue model?

Since teams are how you run businesses, the team slide often goes with business to further establish credibility. When you talk about team, introduce each member's background as it relates to the business. Exclude details of the team that don't relate to the business. If you're the CEO with previous experience managing and scaling teams, share this information. If you also won a math competition, it probably means nothing; so leave it out. If you're a software business, show your team's experience in computer science. If you also have experience in hardware, it probably has no relevance; so leave it out. Provide relevant details that show you'll be successful over other startup teams with a similar idea.

When RidePal began their quest to fund "the Google Bus for the rest of us," a journey that would ultimately lead to half a million in funding, CEO Nathalie Criou gave a great case for her business. Part of her case involved establishing credibility. When Criou presented her team, she explained that everyone on the team had previous startup experience. Their skills included a healthy mix of sales, marketing, development, and product management. Criou then highlighted that her advisors were the very same people who made Google buses successful in transporting commuters around Silicon Valley. Her advisors had done it before, and there was a good chance that they could do it again.

YOU ALSO HAVE THE SUBTLE OPPORTUNITY TO USE ANOTHER PERSUASION TECHNIQUE AND WIN CREDIBILITY: MENTION WEAKNESSES. According to research, when you mention small weaknesses about your company, investors view you as more sincere.[7] Sincerity engenders trust, and trust is a core component of credibility. We know these small weaknesses by another name: business risks. When you take time to reflect on small but real risks and provide plans to mitigate those risks, you show business acumen and persuasive power.

Research suggests that it's good to mention small risks, but what about large risks? Angel investor Clint Korver said that large risks are almost always discovered by investors at some point during the vetting process. If not in the pitch, they will appear when investors do due diligence. If you're caught hiding something, you lose trust. So how do you present a large business risk?

7 K. D. Williams, M.J. Bourgeois, and R.T. Croyle, *The effects of stealing thunder in criminal and civil trials*, *Law and Human Behavior*, 1993, 17: 597-609

WHEN YOU PRESENT RISKS, YOU NOT ONLY HAVE THE OPPORTUNITY TO SHARE RISK MITIGATION PLANS, YOU ALSO HAVE THE OPPORTUNITY TO FRAME RISKS.

For example, let's say you won a large customer like Google. The problem is that Google only used your product once or twice. That sucks. Investors will find this out in the process of due-diligence, and if you led investors to assume Google was an active customer, the gig would be up. However, if you share upfront that Google only used your product a couple of times, you could frame your response as follows: While Google has used the product only a couple of times, we've established a beachhead in the company and are working with their team to design product updates and convert them into an active user.

SEE HOW, BY SHARING THE RISK, YOU CAN REFRAME IT SO THE RISK APPEARS LIKE A BENEFIT?

When you discuss business, be sure you can describe your plans fluently, show how your team complements your business, and divulge weaknesses in a skillful way. By doing so, you establish credibility around your business model. The most important technique is, of course, to make it clear!

Audience Value

Make it interesting. TO WIN YOUR AUDIENCE, POSITION YOUR BUSINESS AS A LOW RISK HIGH RETURN OPPORTUNITY. If you share risks and risk-mitigation plans to establish credibility, you're one step in the right direction. Risk mitigation plans by definition lower the risk.

To show high return, highlight your revenue stream and revenue forecast. If you follow the 4-Point Pitch Formula, you already do this. RidePal compared the costs of their commuter service with the price charged to customers, confirming a healthy gross margin of 60 percent. They also gave a 5-year revenue forecast that amounted to $570 million, a number that would win any investor's heart.

ANOTHER EFFECTIVE WAY TO SHOW BOTH LOW RISK AND HIGH RETURN IS THROUGH TRACTION. The greatest challenge a startup faces is winning customers; when you show traction, you lower the risk that you can acquire customers. You also heighten return because customers are where the money originates. Every entrepreneur knows traction is important. If you have it, show it.

A FINAL WAY TO ESTABLISH AUDIENCE VALUE IS TO HIGHLIGHT STRATEGIC FIT BETWEEN YOUR COMPANY AND THE INVESTORS. One entrepreneur I coached developed a way to enhance the efficiency of solar panels and wondered how he could improve his chance at funding. Since solar is now a commodity industry, few investors are interested in solar tech; however, firms that have a core mission to protect the environment remain receptive to solar technologies. First, I recommended he seek out investors with a compatible interest. Next, research suggests that investors will behave according to their values if you state those values explicitly, so I told this entrepreneur to be explicit in stating the firm's core mission when pitching.[8]

As you know, investors are interested in low risk high return. Share risk mitigation plans, revenue strategy, and traction to show how you make money. Make it interesting!

8 A. M. Tybout and R.F. Yalch, *The effect of experience: A matter of salience?* *Journal of Consumer Research*, 1980, 6: 406-413

Data

Make it real. When you follow the 4-Point Pitch, you have G2M strategies for how to get, keep, and grow customers as well as a revenue model for how you monetize your product. The next step is proof that your strategies and models work. For example, if you introduced a customer acquisition strategy, consider what proof you have that your strategy is effective.

THERE ARE THREE GENERAL METHODS TO PROVE BUSINESS EFFICACY: YOUR CURRENT SUCCESS, MARKET TESTS, AND EVIDENCE FROM OTHER COMPANIES. YOUR CURRENT SUCCESS IS THE STRONGEST PROOF THAT YOUR BUSINESS MODELS WORK.

For example, to prove your distribution strategy works, simply show traction. To prove your loyalty program keeps customers, display customer retention numbers. The best proof comes through your company's success.

To display your company's success, show metrics. After I pitched to AngelPad in 2012, angel investor Thomas Korte tuned me into a set of important start-up metrics that online companies should share when pitching their business – the Startup Metrics for Pirates: AARRR!![9] by Dave McClure, founder of 500 Startups. These metrics include: Acquisition, Activation, Retention, Referral, and Revenue (note the acronym).

Acquisition shows that you're connecting with users and is measured in part through total page visits and time spent on site. Activation shows the depth of involvement by visitors such as multiple clicks and multiple pages visited within the site. Activation also includes the number of customers who signed up for a new account, subscribed to an email newsletter, blog, or RSS feed. Retention statistics involve repeat visits to your site, statistics on the percent of emails opened when you send out newsletters, and email click-through rate. Referral is a measure of whether visitors refer additional visitors. Finally, revenue is plain and simple dollars generated by users. AARRR!

You may want to avoid what Red Room CEO Ivory Madison calls "vanity metrics." A phenomenon identified by Eric Ries, vanity metrics are "accurate but irrelevant" statistics about your business. These metrics are data that look good but carry no business value. Vanity metrics might include Twitter followers, Facebook likes, and other numbers that don't support the bottom line. How many Twitter followers you have doesn't matter, Madison says, it's how many of those followers will click through and buy your product that is useful data. Regarding growth, she says, "Most entrepreneurs are looking at their analytics looking for a number that's growing so they can show growth--no, no Lean Startup for you."

USE METRICS TO PROVE THE EFFICACY OF YOUR BUSINESS PLAN; AVOID PRESENTING METRICS FOR THE SAKE OF PRESENTING METRICS. In the words of Yossi Feinberg, Stanford Professor and head of the popular Stanford Ignite entrepreneurship program, "Present data only when relevant." Don't spill out a bunch of metrics up-front just to look good, because you won't. Metrics need context. Position metrics as proof that your business strategies are successful.

Metrics aren't the only way to show success; you can also share your customers' experiences. CUSTOMER QUOTES AND STORIES PROVIDE INVESTORS WITH THE ASSURANCE THAT YOUR BUSINESS EFFORTS HAVE REACHED AND SATISFIED PEOPLE. RidePal

9 *Sail the vast sea of pirate metrics at http://tinyurl.com/mhh9o3x*

shared customer quotes to support their business success. RidePal even went so far as to share customer feedback on their distribution of commuter stops, explaining how they used this feedback to further develop G2M strategy.

Without solid metrics or customer experiences, you can still support your strategies by sharing business test data. Tests confirm the efficacy of your methods at a minor level. For example, have you run channel tests to prove you can deliver the product to customers? Have you run price tests to prove that customers are willing to purchase your product at your price point? Like a research study, go out and test different price points in controlled experiments. These tests show you've done your homework even though your business might not be fully up and running.

A third way to provide data (i.e., prove) that your business plan works is to reference the success of other companies who are using a similar business model. The more similar the other companies are to yours in terms of product and target market, the more realistic the evidence appears to support you.

Regardless of the data you present, your goal is to convince investors you have a solid way to capture the market and earn money. It may be tempting to dump sheets of numbers on them, but that will only hurt your case. Keep your data simple, clean, and focused on delivering the message that you can do this. When you show data, your business moves from the intangible realm of ideas to the richness of reality. Make it real!

Story

Make it meaningful. Bring your business to life by sharing examples of customer engagements. When DoorDash co-founder Evan Moore pitched his food delivery service to investors, he shared personal anecdotes about running his company. Moore talked about some of the food trips he'd made, funny things that happened between him and customers, and how these events translated into business learning. His stories helped investors experience the business. Share your stories about engaging with customers.

If you have a B2B solution, share business engagement stories such as navigating the sales process with a customer. Engagement stories allow you to illustrate your business in action, emphasize your knowledge of the process, and leave your investors with the perspective of a successful engagement and happy customer.

When sharing stories, your goal is to bring your business to life. Make it meaningful!

SECTION SUMMARY

Credibility

- Be able to talk logically about your G2M strategy and revenue model
- Explain how your team has the skills to run a successful business
- Highlight business risks and risk mitigation plans

Audience Value

- Share risk mitigation plans
- Expand on the details of your revenue model, including gross margin and ROI forecasts
- Show traction
- Emphasize strategic fit with investors

Data

- Share metrics to show the success of your business strategies
- Share successful customer experiences you've had while running the business
- Run market tests to confirm that your business models work
- Highlight the success of other companies using a similar business plan

Story

- Tell anecdotes around successful customer engagements
- Reveal your personal experiences navigating the process of winning customers

EXERCISE: BACK YOUR BUSINESS

1. Identify the qualifications of your team that ensure you can run a successful business.

2. List three business risks you might encounter and how you plan to overcome those risks.

3. Use AARRR! as a guide to collect data that proves the efficacy of your G2M and revenue models.

4. Share a customer engagement story that demonstrates how you navigated a successful customer interaction.

You've now taken big steps to prove you can leverage the market opportunity. Your team shows credibility, risk mitigation plans show audience value, metrics provide powerful data, and your story brings your business to life.

Tailoring Influence

Last chapter you read examples of how to tailor the 4-Point Pitch. Now we examine how to tailor the Elements of Influence.

Tailoring Points

You might ask whether you need to add the Elements of Influence to all four points, Problem-Solution-Market-Business, in your pitch. You don't. Once you've identified the main points of your 4-Point Pitch, those are the points to which you want to bring the most persuasive power. For example, if your pitch is problem-solution focused, you would add Elements of Influence to the problem and the solution. Since market and business are not emphasized, it would not be necessary to make these points particularly influential.

When Stormpulse pitched their weather tracking system in 2011, CEO Matt Wensing breezed through the problem and solution in 26 seconds. He didn't add any influential elements to the problem and solution because he didn't need to convince investors the problem was real or that his solution worked. These were assumed. Instead, he focused his pitch (and his influential power) on market and business. Given his company, this was a great decision.

GOOD PITCHES ARE CLEAR AND SIMPLE. LESS IS MORE. AVOID FLUFFING UP UNIMPORTANT POINTS. DOING SO CAN DISTRACT INVESTORS AND BLUR ATTENTION TO WHAT REALLY MATTERS.

Even so, be prepared to influence investors on any point just in case investors start asking questions. For example, you might not include a deep discussion of your market when you pitch, but investors might start probing your market knowledge through Q&A. Like having backup slides, think of how smooth you'll sound if you can provide an articulate and influential response.

Tailoring Data and Story

If you've gone to pitch events, you probably noticed that investors respond very differently to the same pitch. DIFFERENT INVESTORS DIFFER ON THEIR PREFERENCE FOR DATA OR STORY. Some investors are more analytical while others are more focused on emotional resonance.

When you add influence, I recommend balancing data and story so you can work with any investor. Analytical investors don't want too much emotion, but they're still human and emotions move them to make decisions. Intuitive investors don't require too much data, but they still appreciate proof points.

If you over-focus on data, you lose the ability to motivate investment; if you over-focus on story, you run the risk of damaging your credibility by appearing ungrounded. THEREFORE, BALANCE IS OFTEN YOUR BEST BET WITH INVESTORS.

Consider also what you're most comfortable presenting. If you're an analytical person, you might be more comfortable presenting data. Therefore, you might pitch more effectively by leaning a little more into your data. Conversely, if you're more comfortable sharing stories and customer experiences, you might pitch more effectively by leaning into your stories. YOU WANT TO PRESENT BOTH, BUT LEAN INTO YOUR COMFORT ZONE. INVESTORS INVEST IN YOU, AND THE MORE COMFORTABLE YOU ARE WHEN YOU PRESENT, THE BETTER YOU SHOW UP.

Tailoring for Investment Stage

The elements you include in your pitch also depend on what stage your startup is at. Angel investors differ from VCs when it comes to content. If your company is very young and you're pitching to angels for seed funding, your company won't be in a position to supply data such as strong traction. Seed stage data is often driven by learning and experimentation. Emphasis is on tests you've run rather than market success. Likewise, business forecasts such as ROI and long-term plans aren't necessarily required. Conversely, VCs may need to see more traction in order to reduce their evaluation of investment risk.

SECTION SUMMARY

- Add Elements of Influence into the most important points of your pitch

- Balance data and story so you meet the needs of all investors you encounter

- Recognize that angels and VCs look for different types of evidence

Conclusion

THE ELEMENTS OF INFLUENCE GIVE YOU AN EDGE IN PITCHING. WHEN YOU ADD CREDIBILITY, AUDIENCE VALUE, DATA, AND STORY INTO THE POINTS OF YOUR PITCH, YOU PROVE TO INVESTORS THAT YOU'RE WORTH THE INVESTMENT. MAKE IT CLEAR. MAKE IT INTERESTING. MAKE IT REAL. MAKE IT MEANINGFUL.

By viewing all the content of your pitch through the lens of influence, you can now assess the value of any single piece of information. Why include team? The team furthers the credibility of your business. Why discuss competition? Competition supports your market credibility and can function as market data.

Every piece of content in your pitch, every fact, every feature, every anecdote should act as an Element of Influence. If you share a piece of information but cannot identify what element it is, consider removing it. All the content of your pitch must serve a purpose. The purpose is to prove to investors that your startup is a low risk high return opportunity.

When you pitch to investors using the 4-Point Pitch and Elements of Influence, you can also identify weaknesses in your pitch and fix them. If investors ask for more traction, you can translate that to mean you didn't prove your business plan. Perhaps you really do need more traction, or perhaps you can make your business plan more influential using other data. If investors tell you to work more on your marketing, they're not convinced you can get customers. Maybe you can adjust your acquisition model or use different data points to support your strategy. Conversely if you simply follow the feedback investors provide without understanding the real meaning behind it, you could make dozens of changes to your pitch and still fail to make a single improvement.

Influence isn't magic. If you haven't built up a solid solution or created an effective business strategy, there are no "tricks" that will make you look better. Influence simply helps you show the true value of your startup based on what you've done. If you don't have enough evidence to prove critical aspects of your pitch, this chapter can help you identify the legwork needed before your company is ready for funding.

Use this chapter to help recognize ways to prove the points of your pitch. The ideas presented here are just an outline, they aren't a comprehensive list of possibilities. Remember, this book isn't about business; it's about pitching business. When it comes time to stand in front of investors, this chapter will help you assert confidently that your problem, solution, market, and business are sound and ready for investment.

CHAPTER SUMMARY

• Persuasive presentations include credibility, audience value, data, and story.

• Each point of your pitch is made influential independent of the others.

• Credibility is measured by your knowledge, experience, and clarity when pitching.

• Audience values show your startup as a low risk and high return opportunity.

• Data are facts that verify your words through numbers and real-world examples.

• Story brings out emotional meaning through customer and/or personal experience.

Stormpulse

Hello, my name is Matt Wensing and I'm the co-founder and CEO of a company called Stormpulse. Stormpulse is the world's best real-time weather reporting. Today, when bad weather strikes and lives are on the line and assets and facilities and supply chains are going to be disrupted. Most companies have nothing to turn to other than the weather channel or really expensive meteorologists to tell them how their business is going to be affected by that weather.

← Stormpulse runs quickly through the problem and pains.

But now, they can come to us and get answers to those questions they can't get anywhere else on the internet. That's the product, but what I really want to talk to you today, is about the market. So this market is massive. Every time I think I know how big this market is, another one of this companies reaches out to us, which is what this logos are, and asks us if we can do something for them.

And when they reach out to us, at the top left these represents just a fraction of the thousands of the inbound sales leads that we've have. We have nobody working on marketing except for our premium site, and we see when these people reach out to us, like this Apple logo here. That's not just the guy that fixed your iPhone with the Genius bar, that was actually their Operations Manager who looks over their 3 North American data centers and 400 Apple stores, saying "Hey can you guys do weather alerting for Apple?" We say, "Yeah, yeah we can".

← Note the use of story/anecdote to illustrate market demand. The story also serves as data about the market.

Walgreens, Pepsi, the only thing that most of these companies have in common is that they are on the planet earth, right? And that means, they can't get away from bad weather, which means they can't get away from a need of some kind of weather risk management tool, which is what we do great.

← Indirect reference to market size creates audience value.

So we have a huge market which we're disrupting. And the bottom right-hand corner here we have companies that we have already put in our basket. We sold them some sort of Enterprise Solutions for some part of their business. And again, when FedEx reach out to us, it wasn't the loading clerk guy or the guy at your local store, Kinkos; that was the Managing Director of Global Operations and Command in Memphis saying "Stormpulse saves a lot of time, what else can you do for us?" We said "Yeah".

← Specific reference to customers serves as data.

Frost Banking, Pacific Railroad, the Coast Guard loves us. We're working on a partnership with Bloomberg, you may have heard of them. 7 billion dollars a year on data terminals, and they want to embed Stormpulse in that terminal, they have given us huge opportunities to do that. Yes, even NASA uses Stormpulse.

So my favorite one actually is the White House, it was a classic bootstrapper moment right, I'm standing in my kitchen and pouring cereal which I just bought with last week's pay and pour myself a whatever and I checked my voicemail and it says, "Hi, the White House is calling, we have a question about our Stormpulse subscription, and I said that's gotta be a Google voice mess-up. There's no way the White House called me. Get a call from them, turns out yes the situation room in the White House had called, talked to them, they loved Stormpulse even found a video, which I'm going to show you later of them using it. The White House operations center is obviously the most important Command Centre in the world and when they needed something to do weather awareness, they chose us.

← Story here illustrates (business) traction and offers data.

Ends with a list of audience value, credibility, and data. →

So all these points of three or four or five, let's see how many I get in, amazing things. We have a huge opportunity here. Number one, weather is a long-term trend. It's not going anywhere. Who can escape the weather? Can you escape the weather? Anybody? No, you cannot. Thank you.

Number two, we have a product that's hands-down the best of its kind. There's nothing else on the market like this. It's because we spend 25 thousand hours building it. And we are taking it to market right now.

And number three, we have distribution. We have 3 million people use the site last month. That's these guys. OK, and they're very happy. And they love what we're doing and they want us to do more. So we boot strapped ourselves onto a launch pad and we need your money to launch.

Thank you.

CREDIBILITY + VALUE

+ DATA + STORY

CHAPTER 4

DELIVERY THROUGH DIALOGUE

You will sit in small meeting rooms and talk one-on-one with investors. You need strategies that allow you to interact smoothly with investors as you deliver your pitch.

4. DELIVERY THROUGH DIALOGUE

Presenting in person (Q&A)
Capturing Attention (The Intro)
Delivery
Recognizing results
Getaround's pitch

Chapter 4 Delivery through Dialogue

Every year, Stanford Graduate School of Business hosts a "trial by fire." MBA students role-play as CEOs of small companies and must convince pseudo company board members to support a new business plan. The resistant board members are played by Stanford alumni who fly in from around the world to participate – real CEOs and CFOs of major corporations, presidents of investment firms. These alumni are international influencers, people who roll in the big leagues, own mansions and drive Teslas. Students pit themselves against the executives, and things get heated.

Imagine sitting with the board members of a large company and pitching your business plan to win buy-in. As entrepreneurs, you won't need to imagine this scenario because that's exactly what you do when you walk into meetings with potential investors. It's a high-pressure situation. Investors are experts at dealing with people, they live in mansions and indeed drive Teslas. The good news is there are simple rules that help you tremendously when pitching to them.

As a Stanford communications coach, I judge the communication efficacy of countless students during Stanford's trial by fire (aptly named the Executive Challenge). I also gather feedback from visiting executives and investors on what works and what doesn't during these exchanges. I discovered that student "CEOs" who succeed in convincing board members to adopt their plan almost always develop a good relationship during the discourse. They also use effective presentation devices to drive points home. Through this chapter, you will learn simple strategies to deliver your pitch and win investor buy-in.

Presenting in Person (Q&A)

When I gave one of my first-ever investor pitches to Paul Graham at Y Combinator, I learned the most important lesson in the most painful way possible. As a competition-level presenter, I walked in ready to present like a pro. I had a clean slide deck and a great speech. What I didn't know was that Paul Graham doesn't deal well with one-way conversations. My presentation failed on impact. Graham interrupted me after the first sentence with a tough question, and then another and another. I was so disarmed that I literally didn't know what to say. After the meeting ended, I walked out feeling like a total loser. It was clear we weren't going to receive funding, and the criticisms about our product stung. But it taught me a lesson.

Dialogue

The most important lesson is that every investor pitch is a conversation. When you pitch, you do it through dialogue. RARE ARE THE CASES WHEN YOU HAVE THE FREEDOM TO STAND AS YOU WOULD ON-STAGE AT TECHCRUNCH DISRUPT OR DEMO DAY AND GIVE AN UNINTERRUPTED PRESENTATION. Instead, you will sit in small meeting rooms and talk one-on-one with investors.

ONE-ON-ONE DIALOGUE IS A DANCE BETWEEN POSITIONING YOUR PRODUCT AND RESPONDING TO INVESTOR QUESTIONS AND COMMENTS. Therefore, you need strategies that allow you to interact smoothly with investors as you deliver your pitch.

One effective way to maintain your 4-Point Pitch through dialogue is to view each point of your pitch, the Problem-Solution-Market-Business, as a mini discussion where you're free to maneuver within that point, based on questions and comments from the investor. Once you conclude one mini discussion, you move to the next, perhaps pausing to allow the investor to ask questions before shifting.

Despite its challenges, CONVERSATION BUILDS CONNECTION. Think of conversation as a boon. At the end of the day, investors invest in teams they feel comfortable working with. Shark Tank panelist, investor, and successful entrepreneur Robert Herjavec says, "When I invest, I expect to get my money back, so I'm very involved with my entrepreneurs." Investors don't give you just cash, they give you time. They want to find a team they can work with, and dialogue helps develop that relationship.

THAT'S WHY THE SECOND MOST IMPORTANT LESSON WHEN PITCHING IS TO ORIENT YOURSELF TO BE ON THE SAME TEAM AS INVESTORS.

Being on the same team means being open and receptive to the comments made by investors. During Stanford's Executive Challenge, the single strongest predictor of failure to reach an agreement is when students act resistant or confrontational with board members. The same trend follows on Shark Tank, where Herjavec stars. Resistant entrepreneurs who position themselves against their investors fail to show they can function as a team. If an entrepreneur is resistant or combative to the questions or comments from investors, investors get turned off.

NOW ASK YOURSELF, DO YOU SOMETIMES ACT DEFENSIVE WHEN INVESTORS ASK CRITICAL QUESTIONS? I certainly have. Many entrepreneurs do because pitching to investors can be intimidating. When people feel intimidated, they quickly go into defensive mode and appear resistant. This leads to failure. In the acclaimed negotiation book *Getting More,* Wharton business school professor Stuart Diamond highlights it best: "Adversarial negotiators make about half as many deals as do more cooperative, problem-solving negotiators."

If you feel intimidated, notice your feelings, then consciously adjust your thoughts to move into a receptive team-oriented state of mind.

Answering Questions

Investors invest in people, so they often "kick the tires" of entrepreneurs by asking tough questions to see how well entrepreneurs handle stress.

PART OF HANDLING QUESTIONS IS TO BE RECEPTIVE, AND THE OTHER PART IS SHOWING CONFIDENCE IN YOUR KNOWLEDGE AND CHOICES.

After ZocDoc delivered their pitch in 2007 for an online doctor directory at TechCrunch Top 40, the founders were peppered with comments from the investor panel, including famous persona Guy Kawasaki. Kawasaki appeared skeptical of the idea and commented that he wouldn't go online to find a doctor. The co-founders responded skillfully by saying, "It's an interesting issue that you're raising. What I can tell you is that out of over 100 people we talked to, 90 percent of them all go to their insurance websites to find doctors, and everybody finds it to be a painful process." The co-founders then supported their position with further examples.

When investors query you, pause to consider their words and then answer gracefully and openly. If an investor makes a blunt or discouraging comment, remain receptive as you would when listening to your co-founder or team-member. Investors watch how you react, they see how you relate to them. If investors give you money, they want to be sure their voices will be heard when you spend that money.[1]

Remember also that you know your business better than investors, so after you acknowledge their comment, take steps to support your position. Follow the example of ZocDoc. It's okay to be swayed when the words of investors make sense, but you're just as smart as they are, so stand up politely for what you believe in. Former LinkedIn CEO and VC Reid Hoffman said that successful entrepreneurs "hold onto a vision" and are committed to "the play they are making." When you hold to your position, you show self-confidence and self-direction, qualities of a true leader.

THE MAIN KEY IS TO AVOID BEING DEFENSIVE EVEN IF INVESTORS QUESTION YOUR JUDGMENT. REMEMBER THAT ADVERSARIAL RELATIONSHIPS ALMOST GUARANTEE PITCH FAILURE. YOU DON'T NEED TO AGREE, BUT YOU DO NEED TO SHOW YOU LISTENED AND TOOK THEIR WORDS SERIOUSLY.

When answering questions, concision is particularly important. The more concise your answer, the more you appear knowledgeable and prepared. When ZocDoc fielded Guy Kawasaki's tough comment at TechCrunch, they provided a sufficient response in their first two sentences. The first sentence acknowledged Kawasaki, the second provided evidence to support their position. These little advantages make a large difference in promoting your startup.

1 R.P. Ramsey, and R.S. Sohi, *Listening to your customers: The impact of perceived salesperson listening behavior on relationship outcomes, Journal of the Academy of Marketing Science, 1997, 25: 127-137*

IF YOU FIND YOURSELF IN A SITUATION WHERE YOU DON'T KNOW THE ANSWER TO A QUESTION, TAKE RESPONSIBILITY BY ACKNOWLEDGING THAT YOU DON'T HAVE THE ANSWER AND EXPLAINING WHY. RESEARCH SUGGESTS THAT YOU ARE VIEWED POSITIVELY WHEN TAKING RESPONSIBILITY FOR NOT HAVING ALL THE FACTS.[2] In other words, you actually become more persuasive by acknowledging you don't know! Contrast this to the risk of telling a half-truth and getting caught. Half-truths destroy your credibility; conversely, saying you don't know makes you look good.

Taking responsibility also applies to your company's current status. If investors expose weaknesses in your company such as product flaw or insufficient marketing, take responsibility for your company's situation and respond by explaining how you're overcoming these challenges. Rather than blaming something external like the market, look to the ways your decisions contributed to your company's current status. By taking responsibility, you sound like a leader.

Here are some additional tips when dialoguing with investors: WHEN INVESTORS TALK COSTS, YOU TALK BENEFITS. For example, if an investor points out that your solution has a long manufacture cycle, is expensive, or requires huge resources (costs), explain that a long manufacture cycle provides better durability and will win more lasting customers (benefits). When you convert solution costs into benefits, you gain persuasive power.[3] You also show that you have made thoughtful decisions about your business.

Informed decisions are aspects of leadership, and strong leadership is what drives a company to success.

Finally, honesty and transparency significantly improve your chances for funding. Investor David S. Rose says that the most important quality he invests in is integrity. Investors never invest in someone they don't trust.

When I spoke with angel investor Clint Korver on what people fib about most, he said entrepreneurs frequently inflate their traction. "Ironically," he continued, "traction is one of the easiest things to check." When entrepreneurs say they have customers, investors dig into the details of who those customers are and how they were acquired. Investors might even ask about signed contracts. Once investors start digging, it's very hard to keep up a false story, and they love to dig. IF AN ENTREPRENEUR GETS CAUGHT IN HALF-TRUTHS AND HAS TO BACKPEDAL, THE ENTREPRENEUR LOSES CREDIBILITY.

Because the odds of getting funding are already so low, you can't afford to lose credibility this way.

Instead of fibbing, take responsibility for your status by acknowledging what's true and what's not true. Remember that your acknowledgement of truth often makes you appear better in the eyes of investors.

TRUST IS MORE IMPORTANT THAN TRACTION.

....

2 F. Lee, C. Peterson, and L.A. Tiedens, Mea culpa: Predicting stock prices from organizational attributions, Personality and Social Psychology Bulletin, 2004, 30: 1636-1649

3 G. Bohner, S. Einwiller, H-P. Erb, and F. Siebler, When small means comfortable: Relations between product attributes in two-sided advertising, Journal of Consumer Psychology, 2003, 13: 454-463

Managing Question Topics

When pitching, it's important to maintain your 4-point flow by recognizing the types of questions investors ask and responding appropriately. INQUIRIES HAVE FOUR FLAVORS: PROBLEM QUESTIONS, SOLUTION QUESTIONS, MARKET QUESTIONS, AND BUSINESS QUESTIONS. When an investor asks you a question, identify the flavor of the question and how that fits into your pitch flow.

If the question is unrelated to the point you're discussing, such as a market question while you're still discussing the problem, you can answer the market question concisely and return to the problem; or you can comment that the investor's question will be answered when you discuss the market.

Whatever you do, don't let questions lead the discussion. Avoid getting derailed from your flow by answering a question unrelated to your current point and moving into a full-blown discussion of the new point. For example, if you're discussing the problem and a market question comes up, don't skip the problem/solution and move into a discussion of the market; you would destroy the flow of your pitch and weaken your chances of success. Flow is a critical component to good communication and offers abundant benefits. If questions lead the discussion, you may never get the chance to show investors what they really need to see. YOU ALSO WANT TO MAINTAIN SOME CONTROL OVER THE CONVERSATION SO YOU APPEAR CONFIDENT. However, you can't always plan for the attitude of investors, so use judgment on whether the structure constricts your ability to make a connection. Dialogue is always a dance.

Frequently investors interrupt discussions of the problem and ask entrepreneurs to hurry to the solution. If this happens to you, don't be alarmed. This occurs because entrepreneurs underestimate the knowledge of investors, which leads them to over-supply details that investors already know. If you believe this is the case, oblige and move to the solution. Investors are often knowledgeable about the problem and market because that's where they invest. Remember, they've had dozens of entrepreneurs walk through their door before who explained the same problem and market space.

When investors hurry you through the problem, you can always move the discussion forward to the solution but slip in additional problem details during solution discussion. However, if you have important information about the problem that you must share in order for investors to fully appreciate the benefits of your solution, tell the investors it's important they understand your perspective of the problem, and then continue describing the problem details. DIALOGUE IS ALWAYS A DANCE BETWEEN POSITIONING YOUR GOALS AND FULFILLING YOUR INVESTOR'S DESIRES.

Asking Questions

When conversing, entrepreneurs have a subtle and often underutilized tool: the power to ask questions. Asking questions can help you appear independent as well as orient investors onto your team.

Investors appreciate independence. On his website, Paul Graham writes: "There is nothing investors like more than a startup that seems like it's going to succeed even without them. Investors like it when they can help a startup, but they don't like startups that would die without that help." A self-driven entrepreneur will do everything he or she can to ensure the company succeeds regardless of whether current funding discussions fail. That shows independence.

One way to demonstrate independence is to have investors qualify themselves through asking questions. JUST AS INVESTORS WANT TO DETERMINE WHETHER YOU'RE A GOOD FIT FOR THEM, YOU WANT TO DETERMINE WHETHER THEY'RE A GOOD FIT FOR YOU. WHAT CONNECTIONS OR CACHET DO THEY HAVE TO HELP YOU SUCCEED? ARE THEY ALREADY INVESTING IN THIS INDUSTRY AND WHY? HOW MUCH EFFORT WILL THEY EXPEND TOWARDS YOUR SUCCESS? You want to know these answers for your own success, and by asking them you communicate to investors that you intend to succeed with or without them.

Asking questions can also bring investors onto the same team with you. As we know with dialogue, it's important to situate yourself on the same team. When you ask how investors can support your business, you build a cooperative connection. They begin thinking with you on how to make your startup successful.

To promote team feeling further and increase your influence, query investors' thoughts from time to time. You might ask questions about what's important to them. Do they want to hear more about the market or revenue model? Listen to their input, and adjust your pitch to meet their needs. You can also ask these questions before you meet via email, thereby ensuring your pitch is tailored to their interests.

Asking for feedback or recommendations can also help you gather valuable ideas for your own company. Investors are smart people with perspective. Take advantage of this resource. However, be careful not to ask for so many suggestions that you sound like you don't know your own business.

Finally, questions help you wrap up your pitch. After you finish delivering, ask questions such as what most excites them and how they see your product fitting into their portfolio. When you ask them to recall what they liked most about your pitch, not only does this recall help them convince themselves, you can leverage their answer to go deeper into those details and win their support. Likewise, when investors think of how you fit into their portfolio, they begin thinking of you in terms of their own team.

Conversation allows you to ask questions that move you and investors closer together. Make your pitch a truly balanced interaction by taking time to ask important questions.

SECTION SUMMARY

Dialogue

- All investor pitches are conversations
- Make each point of your pitch a mini-conversation
- Position yourself on the same team as investors

Answering Questions

- Acknowledge investors' comments while supporting your own position
- Take responsibility for not having all the answers
- When investors talk costs, convert those costs to benefits
- Remember that honesty is more important than anything you say

Managing Questions

- Maintain pitch flow by identifying question topics
- Don't let investor questions lead the discussion

Asking Questions

- Ask qualifying questions to show independence
- Query investors for their ideas around your business
- Find out what investors like most about your pitch and focus on those areas

EXERCISE: QUEST FOR QUESTIONS

1. Make a list of questions you might be asked during each point of your pitch. Include some extremely tough and abrasive questions. To help identify questions, look for gaps between what you learned in the last two chapters and what is actually included in your pitch.

2. Make a short list of questions to ask investors about how they can help you develop your business further.

3. Practice asking/answering questions back and forth with your colleagues. Do this for no less than one hour, preferably more. Practice until you're able to deliver answers smoothly and automatically. Be sure that when you answer, you show receptivity to the question asked (particularly the abrasive ones).

Investors invest in you. How you respond to questions has a major impact on an investor's assessment of you. When you practice answering questions effectively through the exercises above, you take a big step towards improving that assessment.

Capturing Attention

You never get a second chance to make a first impression. Nor are investors obliged to listen throughout your pitch. Your most menacing threat in meetings is not your competition, it's cell phones, email, and other distractions that pull investor focus away from you. It doesn't matter what you say if you're not heard. To secure funding, you must secure investor attention. The art and science of presentations provide techniques you can use to enhance your pitch and ensure investors listen to your every word.

The Introduction – Grabbing Attention

When Michael Pritchard began his **LifeSaver** pitch to filter dirty drinking water, he told his audience at the TED conference that they could enjoy the water safely there in England, but local water in many other parts of the world is so dirty that it would give half the audience serious intestinal issues. Pritchard illustrated this fact with a slide of a little girl drinking muddy water from a puddle. The introduction captured the audience and carried their attention through his 10-minute pitch.

WHEN YOU BEGIN YOUR PITCH, INVESTORS GET A FIRST IMPRESSION OF WHAT YOU HAVE TO SAY, AND THIS IMPRESSION COLORS THE REST OF YOUR PITCH.

Grab attention! If you grab attention, investors are more likely to listen to the rest of your pitch even if it slows down. Conversely, if you begin with bland words like "I'm happy to be here, and thank you so much, and what an honor it is, etc.," you spend the rest of your pitch fighting their boredom. You never get a second chance to make a first impression.

One powerful introduction technique is to involve the audience in your pitch. When you begin your pitch by involving the audience in a direct fashion through references or questions, you draw them in and draw their interest. Pritchard's TED intro involved his audience by referencing the water they safely drank that morning and contrasting it to the contaminated water many people had to drink in other countries.

In early 2013, I watched entrepreneurs pitch a personal detection system that gives epilepsy patients an alert if they are about to have a seizure. The team began with a simple problem: "Epilepsy patients don't know when they might lose consciousness; this can be dangerous when they're driving." After the pitch concluded and everyone shuffled out of the tiny meeting room, I took the team aside.

We sat for a few minutes and crafted a new opening. The next time they pitched, they started this way: "Imagine you're driving home from work to have dinner with your wife. One moment you're on the road, then you black out. When you wake up, you're in the hospital hooked to an IV. That's exactly what happens to many people who have epilepsy." The first introduction was clear but boring. Most investors can't grasp what it means to have epilepsy. However, the new introduction involved the investors directly. The problem became personal to them. Grab attention!

Another way to hook your audience is to give them a reason to listen. As we learned in Chapter 1, YOUR PITCH MUST FOCUS ON BENEFITS TO THE AUDIENCE. When Aaron Patzer began his Mint.com pitch at TechCrunch in 2007, he asked the audience if they knew where their money was going. Then he said that everyone in the room would soon discover an extra $1,000 by listening to his pitch. The audience was hooked!

Give investors a reason to listen by sharing benefits or other details that make your company instantly appear like a lucrative opportunity. At the incubator Y Combinator, entrepreneurs are sometimes coached to open their pitch with revenue growth before explaining the problem. Revenue is a benefit to investors that is certain to capture interest. The entrepreneurs are then coached to say that by listening to the pitch, investors will discover how they achieved this revenue growth. Of course revenue is not the only way to start; other details you could begin with include amazing credibility, superior competitive advantage, or information that mitigates investors' main risks around the business.

A third and overarching approach to introductions is to draw audience attention through the use of new, intriguing, or shocking information. When Pritchard began his LifeSaver pitch at TED, he gave a shocking fact about the effects of dirty drinking water around the world by highlighting the number of people suffering and dying from the problem every few minutes. Facts that provide new and unexpected information can draw attention the way television news keeps you glued to your TV set.

Stories are also an effective way to invite intrigue. During Kindara's pitch on Women's fertility technology outlined in Chapter 3, the CEO shared a story about her mother's infertility issues and related suffering. The story was both intriguing and emotional. FACTS AND STORIES, ASIDE FROM BEING POWERFUL PERSUASION DEVICES, ARE GREAT WAYS TO PLUNGE INTO A PITCH.

Some investors recommend beginning your pitch with your elevator pitch. The elevator pitch is outlined in Chapter 2 and provides a short summary of the problem, solution, benefits, and market. A good elevator pitch takes no more than 3 to 4 sentences and orients investors to the rest of your pitch. It also provides you the opportunity to immediately differentiate from other startups with a similar product to your own. When I spoke with famous tech evangelist Robert Scoble, he recommended "you get to something that makes you 10X better than other companies in the first 30 seconds." The elevator pitch is one way to do this.

The techniques above hook investors into hearing your pitch, but the ultimate intrigue hook is the problem you're solving. You've already got that. The problem engages problem-solution thinking, contains an implicit benefit to investors, and can be complemented with intriguing data and story. Therefore, start with the problem and start there fast. Grab attention!

The Overview

After you open your pitch and grab attention, audiences like to have an overview of what you're going to discuss. FOR PRESENTATIONS, THERE'S THE INFAMOUS RULE: TELL THEM WHAT YOU'RE GOING TO TELL THEM; TELL THEM; TELL THEM WHAT YOU TOLD THEM.

Before diving into the bulk of your pitch, tell them what you're going to tell them. Give a brief 1 to 2 sentence explanation of what your pitch is about. This overview signals why audiences should listen to the rest of your pitch. It usually occurs within the first 2 minutes of conversation.

After Pritchard opened his TED pitch of the LifeSaver bottle by involving the audience in the problem, he said, "Today I'd like to show you that through thinking differently, the problem has been solved." This overview explained that the purpose of his pitch was to present a solution to the problem. As Pritchard spoke, his slides showed a picture of LifeSaver's product, giving a hint to his solution. Pritchard then discussed the problem further. Having provided an overview as well as a glimpse of his solution, his audience knew where the discussion would go; this gave Pritchard the freedom to talk about the problem at length without the audience interrupting to ask why.

The overview does not fit neatly into a formula. It can come before the problem, in the middle of the problem, or after the problem. The main aim is to share it within the first 2 minutes of your pitch. LifeSaver pitch was problem-solution focused, and Pritchard wanted to spend time proving the problem. As a result, he first hooked the audience with a taste of the problem; then he gave the overview and continued with the problem. If Pritchard had wanted to focus more on the solution, he could have moved straight to the solution after delivering his overview.

WHEN YOU PITCH, SHARE AN OVERVIEW THAT HIGHLIGHTS THE KEY MESSAGE ABOUT YOUR STARTUP. YOU MIGHT WANT TO HIGHLIGHT THAT YOU HAVE AN INCREDIBLE SOLUTION, MARKET OPPORTUNITY, OR BUSINESS PLAN. For example: After sharing a short introduction of the problem, if the main point of your pitch is that there's a lucrative market, you could say, "We've created a solution to this problem involving xyz technology that allows us to enter a large market." Once investors hear this overview, now they will listen to your pitch, in particular the problem and solution, as context for entering a large market.

Let's look at another example. If the main point of your pitch is to show that you have an exceptional business strategy, you could open with an overview as follows: "This problem creates an obvious market opportunity, and we'll show you how, with the right financial backing, we intend to capture that market." After hearing this overview, Investors now interpret all discussion about the problem, solution, and market as context for delving into your business strategy. This overview also implicitly signals that your purpose of pitching to these investors is to win their financial backing and not to recruit them as advisors.

AN EFFECTIVE OVERVIEW INDICATES THE MAIN MESSAGE OF YOUR PITCH. Consider the key point(s) of your pitch, Problem-Solution-Market-Business, and tell investors within the first 2 minutes what the key point(s) is. When you do, investors have a clear understanding of why you've tailored your pitch as you have.

Holding Attention

Just as you grab attention during your introduction, you want to use techniques to hold attention throughout your pitch. NEW, INTRIGUING, AND SHOCKING INFORMATION GRAB ATTENTION DURING YOUR INTRODUCTION, and you can use this approach anywhere in your pitch to keep things lively. During the delivery of her business about commuter buses in Silicon Valley, RidePal CEO Nathalie Criou introduced a new partnership with Solar City by saying, "We have an announcement to make today." The words announcement and today signaled to the audience that something new was coming, and heads went up to listen. When you deliver your pitch, make it dynamic by using words such as announcement and today to highlight new activities taking place in your company right now. Follow the rule of press and advertising agencies: KEEP YOUR PITCH FRESH WITH CURRENT CONTENT ABOUT YOUR COMPANY. Don't be a litany of facts and historical narrative about your startup. This isn't book-reading — this is news!

Another way to keep content fresh and express relevance is to connect with current events. Peruse newspaper headlines from the last few days and find stories that relate to your industry; then reference those stories during your pitch. For example, Tesla's stock made a huge bounce in May 2013. Anyone pitching clean technology that month could have improved their pitch tremendously by highlighting Tesla's recent market movement. Sue Kwon, Emmy-award-winning storyteller and former head of Social Media at Gap Inc., suggests that IF YOU CONNECT YOUR PITCH TO SOMETHING HAPPENING IN THE NEWS, YOU AMPLIFY YOUR MESSAGE SIGNIFICANTLY.

Emotionally charged words also signal intrigue and excitement that draw in audiences. Steve Jobs was the master of using emotionally charged words. Introducing the iPhone in 2007, Jobs started his pitch at MacWorld saying, "This is a day I've been looking forward to." Later in his pitch, Jobs said the iPhone is "phenomenal" and "way smarter" than any previous phones with a multi-touch technology. When you pitch, grab investors repeatedly by using powerful and emotional words to express your enthusiasm and describe your product.

Vivid descriptions also breathe life into your pitch and breed attention. When Steve Jobs introduced the iPod in 2001, he claimed it could hold your entire music library in your pocket. If you describe your product, experience, or activity using vivid or concrete references, you connect with your audience's personal world and draw them into your words.

A final presentation technique that effectively stuns audiences into attention is to deliver an unforgettable moment. Bill Gates delivered his unforgettable moment during his malaria TED talk by releasing live mosquitos into the audience. Years later, people still speak of this moment with awe.

HOW CAN YOU DELIVER AN UNFORGETTABLE MOMENT WHEN YOU PITCH? THE DEMO. Imagine an exotic situation that illustrates a memorable use for your product. When Pritchard pitched his water filtration technology at TED, he demoed his product by filling a glass tank with river water, sewage run-off, and sheep poop. Then he poured the tainted water into his product, filtered it, and took a drink of the filtered water onstage. Wow. Memorable moments aren't always easy, but they leave an indelible impression. Grab attention!

Emphasizing Your Words

From board rooms to presidential bids, there are three basic speech techniques that enhance specific messages in your pitch. Like a highlighter, they create emphasis. These speech techniques are audience benefits, the power of contrast, and the Rule of Three. You've learned a lot about audience benefits in the previous chapters, so it's repeated here for emphasis. We now bring contrast to the forefront and discuss the Rule of Three as a technique to empower your words.

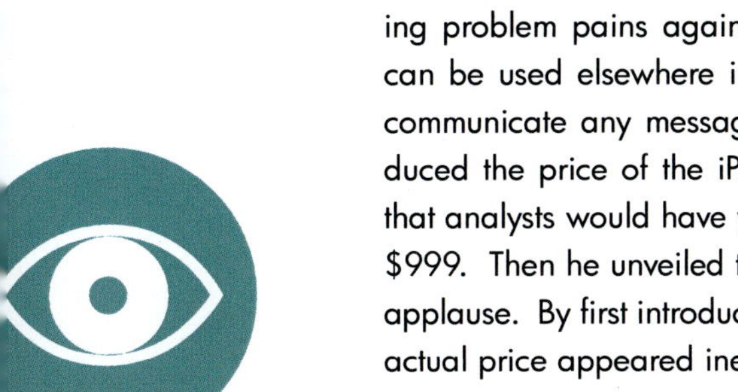

When you introduce the current problem as outlined in Chapter 2, you lay the foundation for contrasting problem pains against solution gains. Contrast can be used elsewhere in your speech to effectively communicate any message. When Steve Jobs introduced the price of the iPad after the demo, he said that analysts would have you believe the price will be $999. Then he unveiled the price at $499 to roaring applause. By first introducing $999 as a baseline, the actual price appeared inexpensive.[4]

You can also use contrast rhetorically to make a lasting impression. One of the most memorable contrasts was made by president John F. Kennedy 50 years ago during his inaugural address: "Ask not what your country can do for you, ask what you can do for your country." This quote remains fresh in our memories while the rest of the speech fades into antiquity.

Rhetorical contrast employs opposing ideas in a single sentence to wow audiences. Obama used simple rhetorical contrast on the Late Show with David Letterman in 2012 when he said that as president, "you got to work for everybody, not just some [people]." The final three words empowered his statement with a contrast and won him applause.

When you use contrast, you illuminate key messages in your pitch so they shine out above your ordinary words and garner audience approval. Rhetorical contrasts such as those used by JFK and Obama account for the majority of applause received during political speeches. It's that powerful.[5]

4 *D.T. Kenrick and S.E. Gutierres, Contrast effects and judgments of physical attractiveness: When beauty becomes a social problem, Journal of Personality and Social Psychology, 1980, 38: 131-140*

5 *J. Heritage, and D. Greatbatch, Generating applause: A study of rhetoric and response at party political conferences, American Journal of Sociology, 1986, 92: 110-157*

Research shows that effective communicators also employ the Rule of Three.[6] THE RULE OF THREE MEANS YOU SHARE THREE THINGS WHEN YOU INTRODUCE A LIST OR TALK ABOUT PARTS. Enigma used this rule extensively in their 2013 grand-prize pitch on public data access.

When Enigma co-founder Marc DaCosta pitched the problem of public data inaccessibility, he described that public data comes in unwieldy structures including "restrictive web portals (1) to messy FTP sites (2) to 1970s database formats (3)." Notice this list contains three examples. DaCosta then delivered his UVP using the Rule of Three by saying Enigma is a "scalable infrastructure for acquiring (1), indexing (2), and searching (3) public data." When co-founder Oudghiri took over to demo the product, his demo was broken into three main sections: comparing data via the example of immigration; discovering data via the example of Google energy; and using Enigma through a web browser. In the end, investors called it a great presentation. When you make lists, limit your sharing to three parts to demonstrate yourself as an effective communicator.

6 *Max Atkinson, Lend Me Your Ears: All You Need to Know about Making Speeches and Presentations (Oxford University Press, 2005)*

Putting It All Together

When GetAround pitched peer-to-peer car-sharing at TechCrunch Disrupt in 2011, CEO Zaid was up against tough competition for the grand prize of $50,000. In his attempt to rise above the competition, Zaid used a combination of attention-holding techniques and words-emphasis. After introducing the problem, Zaid shared that he had three announcements to make today, the first being a new iPhone app. His words employed the Rule of Three while conveying new information. During his second announcement, Zaid introduced a "breakthrough device" that makes car-sharing "hassle free." Notice the way he combined intrigue and benefits. Zaid said this is not "run of the mill ... spaghetti [technology]," it's a device that's "beautiful, low cost, and easy to install." His use of contrast, the Rule of Three, and a combination of emotionally charged words laden with audience benefits was a powerhouse punch that no listener could miss. Co-founder Jessica Scorpio stepped in to conclude the pitch with a memorable moment when she used the app on her cell phone to unlock a Tesla Roadster parked at the back of the conference hall. In the end, GetAround won the $50,000 grand prize with their excellent pitch.

These presentation techniques might appear difficult to implement, but if you follow the pitch structure in previous chapters, you've already done most of the work. Your problem grabs investor attention and sets the stage for contrast against the solution. When you share facts and stories in each point of your pitch, you keep investors intrigued. A significant market serves as an implicit benefit to investors. When you convey passion through words, you hold investors' attention. And when you go all out with your demo, you create a memorable moment. Follow everything you learn in this book, and you will create a powerful pitch.

SECTION SUMMARY

Introductions – Grabbing Attention

- Involve the audience
- Lead with a benefit to investors
- Provide new, intriguing, or shocking info
- Begin with your elevator pitch

Overview

- Highlight the main message of your pitch
- Share the overview within the first 2 minutes

Holding Attention

- Present new, intriguing, or shocking info
- Keep your pitch current with what you're doing now and what's happening in the news
- Use emotionally charged words and vivid descriptions
- Deliver an unforgettable moment during your demo

Emphasizing Your Words

- Share investor benefits at every point possible
- Position important information using the power of contrast
- Recall the Rule of Three when organizing lists

EXERCISE: PRIME YOUR PITCH

1. Create an introduction that involves investors and relates them to the problem.

2. Write a 1-2 sentence overview indicating the main message of your pitch.

3. Open today's paper and find a story that connects with what you're doing. Reference that story in your pitch.

4. Identify two important facts or messages in your pitch. Contrast them as appropriate to make their importance appear even stronger.

5. Notice where you share lists of features and/or benefits. Follow the Rule of Three and organize these lists into three main points.

Pitch tools emphasize important messages and make it easy for investors to follow your words. Don't be afraid to use them generously. Do the exercises again and find even more ways to inject contrast and the Rule of Three.

Delivery

THE SECRET TO GREAT DELIVERY LIES IN ONE INESCAPABLE TRUTH: PRACTICE.

It's been said that Steve Jobs practiced his presentations for two full days before delivery. His speeches contributed to his personal fame as well as Apple's success. If the CEO of a huge company took that much time out of his intense schedule for practice, how much time will you spare out of your schedule?

Practice 1 hour for every 1 minute of pitching. This is the rule I use when delivering a new speech or hosting a new workshop. If stakes are high, practice more. Once while competing in a Silicon Valley speech contest against 1,000 rivals, I practiced a 7-minute speech for 40 hours! (I still only got second place.) I've heard of TED speakers who practice insane numbers of hours too. If you want to be the best against the hundreds of other startups competing for funding, practice no less than 1 hour for every 1-minute of pitching.

Right after DoorDash, a local food delivery service in the Silicon Valley, was accepted into Y Combinator, I asked co-founder Evan Moore how long he practiced. Moore shared with me that before his meeting, the co-founders spent several nights bandying questions back and forth among themselves until their answers were clear and concise. They had already practiced and perfected their pitch in previous weeks for other meetings; this practice was just for Q&A! For Moore, it wasn't enough simply to know the answers; they rehearsed for several hours over several days until the answers were crisp and clear.

Practice is hard and repetitive. As over-achievers, naturally you and your partners don't want to grind through the same pitch 15 to 20 times. You'd rather put that time elsewhere. But pitching is like tennis. One good swing doesn't make a good player. You only get a few chances to jump on the court and win the trophy; don't squander them by avoiding practice. Keep swinging.

How to Practice

PRACTICE ISN'T JUST KNOWING WHAT TO SAY, IT'S SAYING IT OUT LOUD.

When you practice your pitch out loud, not only does your delivery become smoother, you gain two additional and important benefits. First, you hear whether your words make sense when articulated aloud. Writing does not capture the right words to say, and you don't want to sound like a book. I always do my best editing after I hear my speeches aloud. Second — and particularly important whether pitching in front of a large number of people or in a small but high-pressure situation — practice helps overcome nerves.

One afternoon before a pitch event, I sat with a young CEO who was so nervous he almost cancelled his pitch. I had him repeat his 2-minute pitch for 2 hours straight. When he finally stepped onstage, he was still a little nervous but significantly less so. Although he stumbled over a few words in the intro, his practice kicked in almost immediately and he delivered the rest of his pitch with panache.

To improve delivery and reduce your nervousness further, practice your pitch in front of others. If you deliver to real people, you can elicit their feedback. Live feedback is the best way to spot where you might need stronger words or clearer explanation when delivering. Many entrepreneurs practice their pitches at public forums or with a pitch coach to ensure effective delivery. You can also record yourself on video and play it back. When you watch yourself speak, you uncover many distracting habits you never knew existed. Just noticing these habits helps you overcome them at a subconscious level.

PRACTICE DOESN'T MEAN MEMORIZING YOUR PITCH WORD-FOR-WORD. A PITCH IS A DIALOGUE, AND YOU NEED TO FEEL COMFORTABLE ADJUSTING YOUR DELIVERY. You will get interrupted. If you memorize your pitch, interruptions will derail your thinking. Therefore, practice your pitch without reading from a script. Your words might sound a little different each time, but you'll get the point across.

To avoid memorization, I often start my practice with an outline to keep track of the ideas, and eventually I ditch the outline and just practice without any notes. WHEN YOU PRACTICE WITHOUT MEMORIZATION, YOU'LL NOT ONLY BE MORE MANEUVERABLE DURING YOUR PITCH, YOU'LL ALSO SOUND CONVERSATIONAL. WHEN YOU SOUND CONVERSATIONAL, YOU SOUND HONEST AND AUTHENTIC – QUALITIES THAT ATTRACT INVESTORS.

Finally, when you practice, you don't need to repeat your pitch from start to finish every time. One effective method is to practice individual points. Practice delivering the problem. Repeat several times. Then practice delivering your solution. After you feel comfortable practicing the points individually, then you can practice wrapping them together.

Body Language

To ensure connection, maintain eye contact. Successful pitches create connection during delivery. Many entrepreneurs keep their eyes focused on their slides when pitching. This destroys connection with investors and suggests they don't know what's on their own slides. Keep your eyes off the slides and on the investors. EYE CONTACT MAKES THE CONVERSATION APPEAR MORE INTERESTING AND MORE PERSONAL. EYE CONTACT ALSO GIVES YOU THE ABILITY TO WATCH INVESTORS' REACTIONS AND TO ADJUST YOUR PITCH BASED ON THEIR BEHAVIOR. If they get bored, you might ask them a question or move through the current topic more quickly. If they show interest, you might go deeper into the details. Remember that in conversation, it's natural and expected to look at the person you're talking with.

How about other aspects of delivery like body movement and voice? Do you lean in or out? Should you speak loudly or softly? The answer is you don't need to worry about it. When you have a conversation, your body and voice naturally modulate to connect with investors, just as they do in any conversation. The more you practice, the less your nervousness interferes with your natural behavior. Even when you're onstage at a major event, practice ensures your delivery appears natural, confident, and expressive.

Many excellent investors aren't looking for slick presentations, they're looking for sincerity. Let practice be the foundation of sincere delivery and connection, and you will stand out from the crowd.

SECTION SUMMARY

How to Practice

- Practice your pitch for at least 1 hour to each 1 minute of speaking
- Practice your pitch out loud
- Do not memorize your pitch

Body Language

- Maintain eye contact

EXERCISE: PRACTICE PITCHING

In previous chapters you've created drafts for each of your points. Pick a point, perhaps your problem, and now deliver that point without using notes for an hour straight.

This one hour will change your entire perspective on how much better practice makes you sound. Even though you know exactly what to say before you practice, it won't come naturally to your mind; you'll hesitate as you speak; you might even forget important facts. By the end of the hour, your words will flow naturally without notes.

Recognizing Results

Good meetings end with follow-up meetings. There's a process to winning investment, and the goal of your pitch is to proceed through this process. Your first meeting might be with an associate at a VC firm. If you do well, you'll have the opportunity to pitch to a partner. If the partner pitch succeeds, you'll probably pitch to other partners in the firm including the general partner. Therefore, victory comes in the form of follow-up meetings.

As you advance through the pitch process with VC firms, investors will set up meetings for "due diligence" to corroborate the data you presented as well as examine your startup in-depth. Due diligence might include detailed discussion about your product, closer examination of the market, and review of your finances. This is a great thing. IF INVESTORS ARE WILLING TO GREASE THEIR ELBOWS LOOKING AT YOUR STARTUP ACTIVITY, THEY ARE CLEARLY INTERESTED IN YOUR COMPANY. The upside of due diligence is that you can keep your message simple when you pitch and avoid deep diving into analysis. The downside is that if you fibbed while you presented, you'll probably get caught. Just another reason to be honest!

If investors are not interested in pursuing a follow-up meeting, and this happens to everybody, ask for names of other investors who might be interested. There are several reasons why investors might reject you that have nothing to do with your startup. Perhaps the investors are not ready to enter your industry; or maybe they're already invested in a similar startup. Whatever the case, make your meeting a success by walking away with information that can help you move closer to winning funding.

Conclusion

Every pitch is a conversation, and this dialogue is a dance with many benefits. It allows you to connect with investors, show listening and leadership skills, and ask questions that confirm your conviction. When you enter the meeting room, you'll be prepared now with the right mindset to move fluidly between your pitch and the concurrent conversations that will inevitably take place.

During you pitch, captivate investors with techniques that grab and hold their attention. Make your first impression count; then provide an overview so investors know what to listen for. As you progress through your pitch, keep it current.

The success of your pitch and your conversation will depend on one simple truth: practice. The more you practice delivering your pitch and answering questions, the more effective will be your presentation. You've taken months to prepare your product for funding, you've taken the time to read this book, now take the time to practice. I assure you, it takes longer to arrange investor meetings than it does to prepare for them. Once you have a meeting scheduled, do everything in your power to make it a success.

CHAPTER SUMMARY

- All investor pitches are conversations
- Orient yourself on the same team as investors
- Practice answering and asking questions to succeed in conversation
- Maintain investor interest through grabbing and holding their attention
- Use presentation techniques such as contrast to emphasize your key messages
- Practice, practice, and more practice

Getaround

2011 TechCrunch Winning Pitch

Good afternoon TechCrunch. My name is Sam Zaid, I'm the CEO of Getaround. With me on stage are my co-founders, Jessica Scorpio and Elliot Kroo. We're here to share our vision for solving a problem we call car overpopulation. We have over 250 million cars in America, that sit parked 22 hours each day.

Our solution to this problem is Getaround. A *new way* for people to share cars. Instead of buying a car, you can rent one instantly from someone nearby. And as a car owner, you can earn thousands of dollars a year sharing your car. ←

Today, we redefine car ownership with 3 *amazing announcements*. The first, a *powerful new* iPhone app, Jessica please take it away.

Notice italicized words like "new" and "announcement" keep it it current. Charged words like "amazing" and "powerful" heighten emotion.

Thanks Sam. Getaround is a marketplace for peer-to-peer car sharing. The airbnb for cars. Owners have pricing and availability, Getaround provides insurance and takes a 40% commission. Just a few months ago, we launch an exclusive trial in San Francisco. And now it has expanded all over the Bay Area. ←

Here is the UVP followed by a tagline.

This is why Getaround is so *disruptive*. The peer-to-peer model is not limited to dense urban areas like Zipcar. Here in Nob Hill, on the map, Sally shares her 2006 Volkswagen Beetle for $5.50 an hour and $33.50 a day. In Soma, Trung shares his 2010 3-Series BMW for $15 an hour, and $60 a day. Let's check out this BMW. ←

Shortly after the UVP comes the demo, told as a story.

As a renter, I can see who owns it, where the car's located, when it's available, car features and *beautiful* photos uploaded by the owner.

Ratings and reviews help me filter for *beautiful* cars and great people. If this car looks good, hit Request. Select the Start Time and End Time and confirm the rental. Once the owner confirms the request, you get a key on your iPhone app. With it, you can unlock the car and locate the car. All from your iPhone.

The Getaround iPhone app available for free on the App Store *today*.

So, we're not done. OK. (There's more.) So, how can an iPhone app unlock your car? The answer is, our second *announcement* of the day. A *breakthrough* device, that makes peer-to-peer car sharing hassle-free. Now, this is not your run-of-the-mill fleet management spaghetti like you're seeing here. This is a *beautiful*, low-cost and easy to install device that combines a keyless remote with WiFi and GPS. ←

GetAround uses contrast and Rule of 3 to make their device sound golden.

We call it the Getaround car kit. The *first ever* device designed to securely share access to your car, using only a smartphone. You can even install it yourself. Takes less than 5 minutes. So we're going to be giving away the first 500 of these for free. And if you like one, then sign-up at Getaround.com.

Our third and final *announcement*, answers the question that everybody asks. How does insurance work? Getaround provides insurance as part of each rental. *Today*, we're *excited to announce* that we've secured a unique

GetAround establishes credibility in their business by mentioning Berkshire Hathaway. →

deal with an *amazing* insurance carrier that will help us expand our coverage across the entire country. That carrier is Berkshire Hathaway. One of the *most trusted* names in insurance. Let's review.

The Getaround iPhone app. The Getaround car kit. *Super-safe* insurance provided by Berkshire. 3 *amazing announcements* that redefine car ownership. But, can we actually solve car overpopulation?

For a moment, imagine 1 million shared Getaround cars. We'd have taken 10 million cars off the road. CO2 emissions would drop by a *whopping* 48 billion pounds per year. Which is like planting a billion trees. Zip car with 8,500 cars is a billion dollar company. We'd be 100 times bigger.

This may sound like a pipe dream, but remember there are over 250 million cars in America. Sharing 1 million cars, means sharing less than half of 1% of all the cars we already own. If you like what you hear, sign-up at Getaround.com. Sign-up is free, and there are no membership fees. On behalf of the whole Getaround team, myself, Elliot and Jess. Where's Jessica? Jessica? Oh Jess, what you're doing over there?

Ends on a memorable moment—demoing their app to unlock a Tesla Roadster. →

Sam, hello. I'm not sure Elliot tested the iPhone app before pushing it to the App Store, so I'm gonna test it here and now. (OK.) Here we go. Lock. Unlock. Looks like you can pay Elliot this week Sam. The Getaround iPhone app, download it, we can help you get around.

CHAPTER 5

STRONG SLIDE DECKS

Slides aren't your pitch, slides support your pitch. If done right, your words won't add value to the slides; the slides will add value to your words.

5. STRONG SLIDE DECKS

Chapter 5 Strong Slide Decks

If you ever meet an entrepreneur who built his or her pitch from a slide deck, smile. If this entrepreneur is pitching to the same investor as you, you're the one who's going to win funding. No investor ever invested money in a slide deck. Investors invest in you.

When you pitch to investors, your goal is to rise to the center of attention. Slides can help you stand out by clarifying ideas and enhancing memory recall, or they can distract investors from listening to your well-thought out words.[1] Many entrepreneurs, weak in their words, lean on slides and lose everything.

SLIDES AREN'T YOUR PITCH, SLIDES SUPPORT YOUR PITCH.

The best slide decks are created after you write your pitch. If done right, your words won't add value to the slides; the slides will add value to your words.

In this chapter, we take a high-level look at the slide deck, and then we delve into choosing the right slides for your pitch. Finally, we review some basic tips for slide design. Whole books are written on slide design, but the goal here is for you to learn as much as you can in as little time as possible. When you're done, you will see slides from a very different and far more useful perspective.

1 *Robert Lane and Stephen Kosslyn, Show Me! What brain research says about visuals in PowerPoint, http://office.microsoft.com/en-us/powerpoint-help/show-me-what-brain-research-says-about-visuals-in-powerpoint-HA010277194.aspx*

The Slide Deck

You probably have a lot of questions about your slide deck. Because startup tradition teaches erringly to design pitches around slides, many of these questions seem more important than they really are. However, here are answers to the most frequent inquiries.

One common question is: DO YOU PITCH WITH THE SAME DECK THAT YOU EMAIL TO INVESTORS? The answer to this first question is a resounding NO! Peter Thiel, one of Forbes' top 10 tech investors in 2013, recommends having two decks: The first deck to be emailed, info-rich, and the second deck to be presented live. This chapter focuses on designing the live deck you deliver at your meeting. At the very end of the chapter there are a few notes on the deck you send through email.

How many slides do you include in your live deck? The best advice is Guy Kawasaki's famous 10-20-30 rule. Kawasaki recommends using 10 slides delivered in 20 minutes with 30-point font. Ten slides is a good guideline because it prevents you from delivering too many slides and confounding your message; however, slide count can vary on either side of this average.

If we look at the slide count of successful pitches onstage, here's what we see: Kindara used 8 slides in 3 minutes; Enigma used 9 slides in 6 minutes; and ZocDoc used 5 slides in 7 minutes. In other words, there are several roads to Rome. Don't feel obliged to force your slide deck to a certain length. The main goal is to keep your pitch focused by using only the necessary slides to convince investors of your investment value.

Finally, what slides do you include in your deck? Startup tradition would have you include a team slide, a competition slide, even a product slide. However, I've seen pitches win without these. When Enigma won the grand prize at TechCrunch Disrupt in 2013, they didn't have a team slide. Neither Enigma nor the now-funded RidePal had competition slides when they pitched. And many successful pitches don't even bother with a product slide (instead, these companies show demos).

Effective Slides

Before we can answer what slides to include in your pitch, let's look at what it means to have effective slides. Sun Microsystems co-founder and VC mogul Vinod Khosla uses a 5-second rule to assess the quality of slides.[2] First, he puts up a slide for everyone in the meeting room to see. After 5 seconds, he takes the slide down and asks someone in the room to explain what the slide was about. If the person can't understand and explain the slide after looking at it for five short seconds, it fails the 5-second rule. It's not clear.

THE CARDINAL RULE OF SLIDE PRESENTATION IS TO PRESENT CLEAR SLIDES. THE BEST WAY TO DO THIS IS TO HAVE ONE MESSAGE PER SLIDE. When Enigma delivered their winning pitch, their opening slides outlined the problem. One slide title read, "Why public data is broken." The next title read, "You can't search for public data," followed by "You can't discover and connect data sources." The slides progressed logically, creating a natural flow. Even more important, each slide focused on only one message. If you include more than one message in your slide, you confuse your audience.

SUCCESSFUL PITCHES USE EACH SLIDE TO CONVEY A MESSAGE SUPPORTING ONE OF THE 4 PITCH POINTS: PROBLEM, SOLUTION, MARKET, OR BUSINESS. When Michael Pritchard pitched his amazing LifeSaver water bottle at TED, his first slide showed a little girl drinking muddy water from a puddle. The slide had no title but the image conveyed the problem. Shortly thereafter, he presented a slide showing a glass of crystal-clear water and a picture of his water bottle in the background. Problem-solution.

When choosing what messages to highlight in each point, focus on your Elements of Influence: credibility, audience value, data, or story. For example, Pritchard's picture at TED of the little girl drinking muddy water conveyed emotions to support the story of the problem. His solution slide of clear water showed data on what his technology could do. Research suggests that when you present information with visual aids, it becomes 43 percent more persuasive than without visual aids.[3] Use this power to push influence.

2 *Vinod's rule: http://www.forbes.com/sites/jerryweissman/2011/10/26/vinod-khoslas-five-second-rule/*

3 *D. R. Vogel, O.W. Dickson, and J. A. Lehman, Persuasion and the role of visual presentation support: The um/3m study, 1986, http://misrc.umn.edu/workingpapers/fullpapers/1986/8611.pdf*

Returning back to the original question: WHAT SLIDES DO YOU INCLUDE IN YOUR SLIDE DECK? The answer: It depends. If your pitch is market-business focused, you would present slides to prove the market and business. For example, you could include a competition slide as data on the market; and you could introduce a team slide to drive credibility into your business. Although you might include 1 or 2 slides about the problem and solution, these points (and slide attention) would be downplayed.

Backup Slides

Backup slides are the slides you do not intend to show during your pitch. These slides aren't there for you to use randomly on a whim; you want to be more prepared than that. Backup slides are there when you need to adjust your pitch based on investor comments and questions.

The most likely time you might adjust your pitch is when investors dig deeper into your pitch points. When you tailor your pitch, you emphasize certain points like the problem and solution, and you de-emphasize other points like the market and business. You might include a few backup slides to support data around your main points if investors dig there. However, backup slides are particularly important when investors start digging into your de-emphasized points. If you only show one slide on the market and investors start hammering for more market details, imagine how great you'll look if you can smoothly pull out a set of slides to prove your market.

SECTION SUMMARY

- Create two decks: one to present in person and one to email
- Keep your in-person slide deck short with roughly 10 slides

Effective Slides

- Design each slide to communicate one message
- Design messages to support one of the 4 Points: problem, solution, market, or business
- Ensure messages add influence through credibility, audience value, data, or story

Backup Slides

- Create backup slides to provide further data around your main points
- Create backup slides to add influence around your non-main points if necessary

EXERCISE: OUTLINE THE SLIDE DECK

1. Recall the two or three main points you identified while tailoring the 4-Point Pitch. Identify at least one important message from each of these main points that you want to convey to investors.

2. Assess whether each message is best supported through showing credibility, audience value, data, or story.

You now have a rough outline of the important messages to emphasize in your slide deck. These messages will help you choose the right design for each slide.

Slide Design

You don't need to be an artist to design great slides. T.S. Eliot, one of America's best-known poets, said, "The most important thing for poets to do is to write as little as possible." When you design slides, your most important skill is not your artistic talent; it's your ability to convey the message in as few details as possible. Less is more.

SLIDES ARE MEANT TO REDUCE COMPLEXITY, NOT INCREASE IT.

If you design complex or overly detailed slides, investors must take time to interpret each slide. Realistically, this means investors will do one of two things: they either ignore your slide in order to hear what you say; or they ignore what you say in order to read your slide. In the words of Presenting to Win author Jerry Weissman: either way, you lose.

To keep your slides simple, here are some design tips on the use of images, numbers, and words.

Image Slides - Photos

IMAGES ARE THE MOST POWERFUL TOOL IN YOUR SLIDE DESIGN ARSENAL.

In the words of slide gurus Robert Lane and Harvard Professor Stephen Kosslyn: "Not all visual stimuli are created equal. Some cruise through our neural circuitries with ease and others require more analysis. Text is a prime example of the latter. Asking people to read text on slides requires a lot of processing effort.... Appropriate images, on the other hand, require relatively little processing because they fit with the message." Minimize the burden you put on investors by using images that fit with your message.

You can use images in the form of photographs to convey emotion. The slide below comes from Village Help for South Sudan, an organization that runs projects for underserved communities in Sudan that include infrastructure developments for poor villages.[4]

If you were to share the problems South Sudan villagers face, this photo would add immeasurable power to your story. Notice how the sole focus of the slide is a boy drinking dirty water from a bucket. It brings the problem to life.

When you use photos, limit yourself to one photo per slide. People respond mentally and emotionally to one photo, but if you add an additional photo, the

4 *Learn more about the amazing projects of Village Help for South Sudan: http://villagehelpforsouthsudan.org/*

experience gets muddled. It's like trying to watch two movies on one screen; you end up disengaged from both of them. More photos create less meaning; less creates more. The same rule applies with words.

Avoid adding words to your photo slides. Look what would happen if you added words.

By adding words, the slide loses emotional power. The words distract from the image and require you to do mental work. Mental work certainly doesn't make it easier to connect emotionally. Let your voice say the words and let the slide carry the photo. This way you achieve maximum impact.

The most effective use of photos is to complement stories, but you can also use photos to show your product in use or divulge other glimpses of reality that bring your words to life. Overall, photos pack a powerful punch.[5]

5 *Watch LifeSaver pitch to see great use of photos: http://www.ted.com/talks/michael_pritchard_invents_a_water_filter.html*

Image Slides - Icons

Images can also be used to clarify your words and help your audience follow along. To do this, use icons. Let's say you want to discuss 3 key ideas around your solution, for example: security, energy, and the environment. You could use the slide below to make your categories clear to investors.

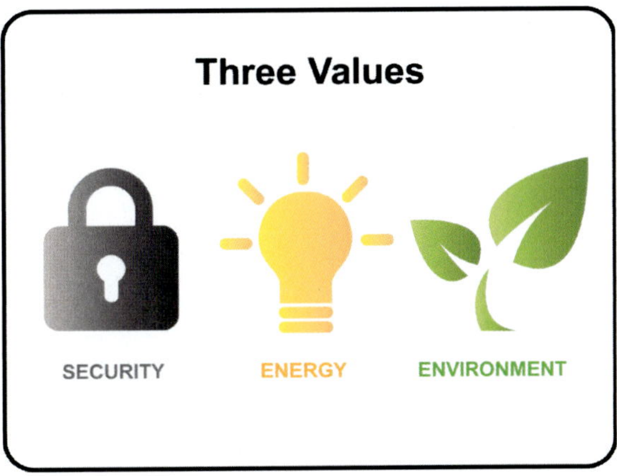

Likewise, if you want to share a complex idea, use icons to add a visual component to your concepts so the audience can keep track of the discussion.

When you use icons, be sure to display no more than 4 icons at a time.[6] The slide above uses 3 icons, making it easy for the audience to quickly orient themselves to your words. If you were to use 5 icons, the audience would become overloaded.

DON'T ADD COMPLEXITY BY DISPLAYING A DOZEN IMAGES. LESS IS MORE.

If you need to display more than 4 icons on a slide, uncover the images in sequence. For example, you might first show only 1 or 2 icons. Once the audience has had a moment to process them, you could uncover the next icons. In this way, the audience is never hit with more than 4 icons at a time. Of course, if you're planning to design a slide with more than 4 icons, maybe it's best to consider first whether you can make the slide simpler.

6 *Stephen M. Kosslyn, Clear and to the Point: 8 Psychological Principles for Compelling PowerPoint Presentations, (New York: Oxford University Press, 2007); and N. Cowan, The magical number 4 in short-term memory: A reconsideration of mental storage capacity, Behavioral and Brain Sciences, 2000, 24: 87-185*

You can also use icons to create diagrams that show relationships between ideas or illustrate a process. For example, if you had a product that collected rainwater, filtered it, then distributed it to farms, you could use the slide below to illustrate the process.

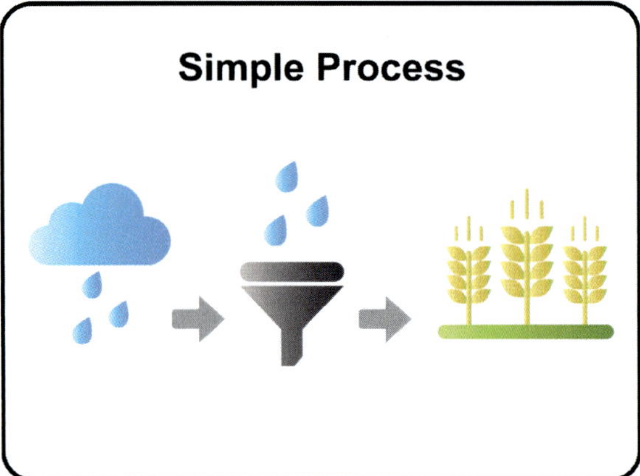

You might consider drawing a diagram to illustrate complex business models. For example, if you wanted to map out the sales process to your customers, you could use icons to represent each stage of the process and add connecting lines between the icons to show process flow.

Just like normal icon slides, effective diagram slides introduce no more than 4 icons at a time. If you were to display a process that has more than 4 stages, you might consider uncovering the stages in sequence so the audience can follow you more fluidly.

Icons and diagrams display ideas and make it easy for the audience to follow your words. Use them to clarify complexity.[7]

7 *Watch Enigma's pitch to see great use of icons: http://techcrunch.com/2013/05/01/and-the-winner-of-techcrunch-disrupt-ny-2013-is-enigma/*

Number Slides

Almost all entrepreneurs will display number slides to support their data. Unfortunately, most entrepreneurs tend to make at least 1 of 3 common mistakes:

1. They display data without a clear message, forcing investors to interpret the data.
2. They show numbers without formatting, making it difficult to decipher the data.
3. They display more than one chart, adding complexity by having competing points.

Look at the all-too-common spreadsheet slide below:

Revenue

	Q1. '15	Q2. '15	Q3. '15	Q4. '15	Q1. '16	Q2. '16	Q3. '16	Q4. '16
REVENUE	**450**	**460**	**470**	**480**	**590**	**600**	**610**	**620**
Room Revenue	200K	210K	220K	230K	240K	250K	260K	**270K**
Conference Revenue	100	100	100	100	200	200	200	200
Restaurant Services Revenue	150	150	150	150	150	150	150	150
COSTS	**240**	**240**	**240**	**240**	**240**	**240**	**240**	**240**
Upkeep Costs	10	10	10	10	10	10	10	10
Furnishing	2	2	2	2	2	2	2	2
Rent	150	150	150	150	150	150	150	150
Labor								
Housekeeping Supplies	4	4	4	4	4	4	4	4
Laundry	4	4	4	4	4	4	4	4
Service	40	40	40	40	40	40	40	40
Reception	30	30	30	30	30	30	30	30

What's the message? It's not clear without help. If you have to explain your slide, the focus moves from you to your slide. Investors don't invest in slides. Perhaps the message is that revenue grows over time while costs remain flat.

You could highlight the revenue and cost rows to make your spreadsheet more clear, but better to reorganize the data like this:

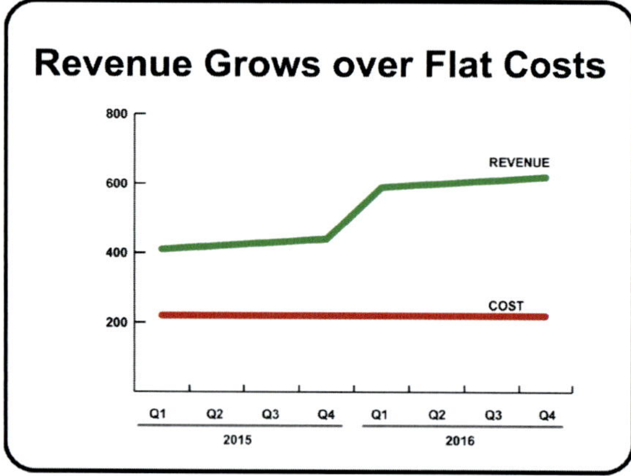

When the message is clear, the slide supports you. To make graphs and charts easy to read, display only the minimal details on x and y axes, data labels, etc. required for the chart to be understood. Graphs make numbers clear; be sure to keep your graphs clear too.

Let's return to the spreadsheet. What if the message was actually that gross margin will be 60 percent by the end of 2016? You could highlight the Q4'16 cells in the spreadsheet, but that still leaves your slide cluttered with a bunch of extra unnecessary numbers. The important goal is to convey a clear message.

Why not display the data like this instead.

60% GM by 2016

Revenue	$620,000
Costs	-$240,000
Profit	**$380,000**

You might resist this format. You might think that investors want to see the whole spreadsheet to confirm you've done your homework. Not so! Your pitch is not a math lesson. Send the spreadsheet by email or wait until there's a follow-up meeting for investors to perform due diligence. Sure, you want to be able to talk about expenses and revenue; but don't show it. During your pitch, convey clear messages.

To display data effectively, organize your numbers into a graph, chart, or simple table with a clear message. I've coached many startups that try to make their data visual but don't quite succeed. Below is the slide designed by one startup I coached.

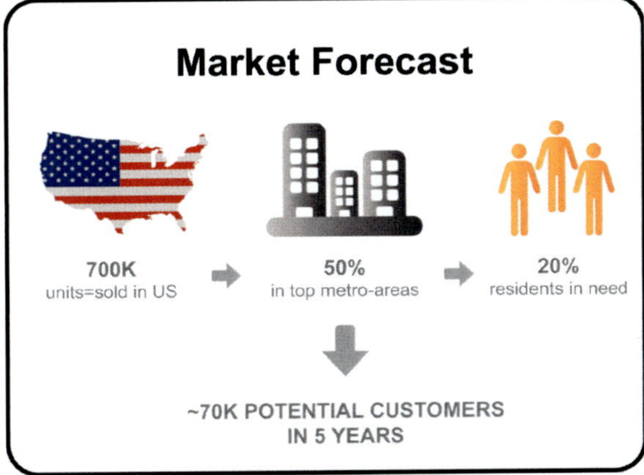

This slide was a math lesson that buried the message. After organizing the numbers into a single pie chart and reducing the text, we were able to make the message clear. In general, pie charts display relative amounts (percentages), bar charts compare values, and lines show trends. Notice the difference as simplicity emerges.

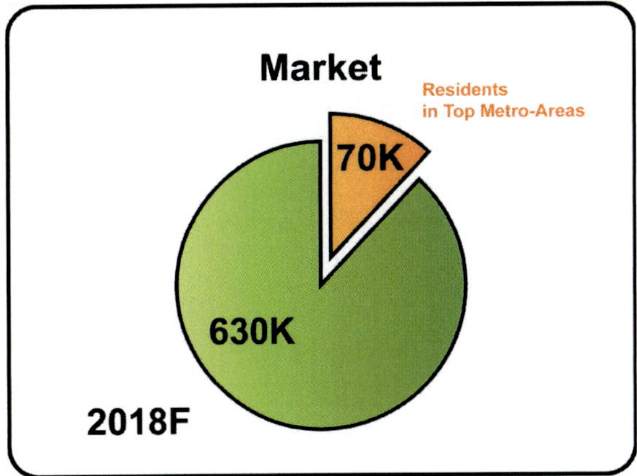

When you clarify your data, use only one chart per slide. Two charts, like two pictures, split attention and convey no message. While hosting a workshop on pitching for Stanford post-docs, I once had a participant show me a slide with six pie charts. Six! Each chart represented different data about his customers. When I asked what it all meant (I couldn't figure it out), he said it meant we needed to change things. What he didn't realize was that it wasn't his customers who needed changing, it was his slide.

Many entrepreneurs don't take the time to clarify their data. They tend to make the mistake of displaying data without a clear message, displaying data without formatting, or displaying more than one chart. Avoid these pitfalls by organizing data into a single chart, graph, or table with a clear message that jumps out at the audience. Good data slides force a conclusion in the minds of investors.

Word Slides

Word slides seem like a skeleton key to slide decks. With words, you can convey literally anything in your slide. As a result, many professionals from all walks of life use them extensively. As it turns out, word slides are probably the least effective slide in your design arsenal. Why? Because research shows that it takes mental effort to process words. Why else? Because you don't want slides to speak for you. You want to be the one to deliver information. Investors invest in you. Don't let the slides do the talking.

There are two common types of word slides: quotes and description. Quotes are easy. Write quotes verbatim with the source listed underneath.

Entrepreneurs run into trouble when they start using slides to describe ideas like this.

Description

- Our widget provides a long-term sustainable way for people to water their plants
- The app provides reminders of when to water
- The price is only $5.99
- It is scientifically based off years of research
- We are launching to all mobile platforms with the same price regardless of which platform is used

Take a moment to consider what's wrong with this slide above.

Now let's analyze it. First, there are a lot of words - 53 to be exact. This fails the 5-second rule. If the average person reads 3 words per second, they have no chance of processing 53 words in 5 seconds. Okay, what else? The more words on the slide, the more mental effort it takes. Even if there were only 15 words, it would still require considerable effort for investors to read. Why force investors to take maximum mental effort during those 5 seconds?

Let's keep analyzing. Some bullets wrap around to a second line. WRAPPED LINES LOOK UNPROFESSIONAL AND REQUIRE EFFORT BY THE AUDIENCE. The audience must flash their eyes back and forth across the screen multiple times just to capture one concept. Finally, the worst part of this slide: The slide speaks for the presenter. Why is the slide saying what the product does? This is the speaker's job. Investors don't invest in slides, they invest in you.

When you put up a slide like this, you either force investors to ignore the slide and listen to you; or you force investors to ignore you and read the slide. Word slides are dangerous. So how can we make this slide better?

First, let's focus on an influential message that matters. In this case, descriptions can be removed because the presenter will speak them. That leaves us with a set of features. We can either convert those features into more clear and relatable phrases, or we can convert those features to benefits.[8] After some tinkering, we might come up with this.

Top Features

- Proven process
- Half the cost of competitors
- Any mobile devices

Lists are perhaps the best use for word slides. When listing items, keep the list short and use only a few words per line. Never let a bullet point wrap around to a second line. When former CEO and Mozilla Chairwoman Mitchell Baker gave her keynote to TechCrunch Italy in 2012, she listed the following qualities of an open web that Mozilla desired to take into the mobile environment:

- Interoperability
- No advance permissions
- Distributed
- Content neutral

Effective lists use minimal words per line. Throughout Baker's presentation, most phrases on her slides were extremely short. This made it easy for the audience to absorb quickly.

SO HOW DO YOU KEEP BULLETS SHORT? If you're listing features or benefits, stick to key adjectives. Don't write full-sentences. Imagine if Baker had written: the open web has interoperability; the open web requires no advance permissions; it is distributed; all

8 Presentations Author Jerry Weissman says that listing features on slides is fine as long as you convert those features to benefits in your narrative.

content is neutral. What a waste of words. Listing adjectives only keeps it clear. You can also make lists of nouns and verbs; the key take-away is to avoid full sentences.

Display a maximum of 4 bullets at a time. We know that humans can only take in 4 new images at a time, so consider each bullet to be one image. You can use longer lists; but if you do, uncover the bullets in sequence. This technique was used by Steve Jobs. When Jobs presented the first iPad in 2010, he listed 7 requirements for the new iPad to be successful. On his slide, he started out by displaying only the first bullet: browsing. Jobs gave a brief comment about the importance of web browsing. He then uncovered the next bullet: email, gave another brief comment, uncovered the next bullet, and so forth. When you deliver long lists, give your audience the chance to absorb the list by uncovering one bullet at a time.

Let's look at another very typical word slide: the team.

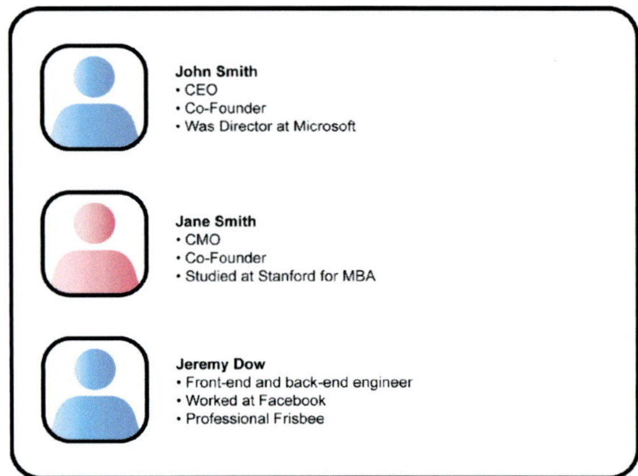

What's wrong with this slide? First, there are 30 words. Second, what's the message? If you're displaying a team slide, you want the clear message to be that your team can run the startup. The purpose is credibility.

Here's how we might revise the slide to focus on what matters:

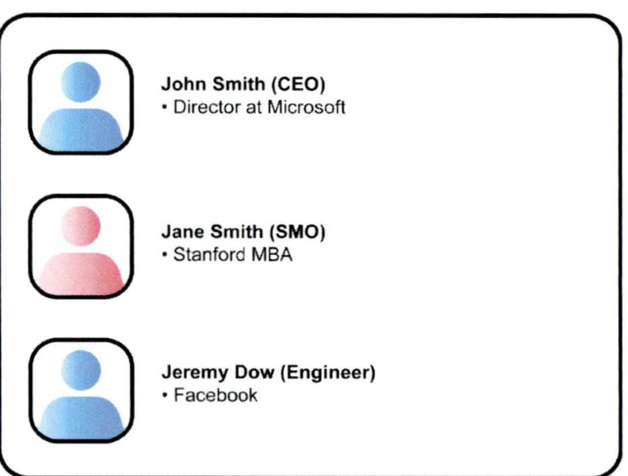

Unnecessary descriptions like "professional Frisbee" have been removed. The co-founders will (hopefully) have introduced themselves and do not need to be re-introduced on the slide. Bullets have been shortened to focus on keywords.

After making edits, now the details that really matter pop out. The CEO has previous management experience; the business person has an MBA; the engineer worked at an established company. The slide becomes powerful.

Word slides are versatile, making them great for function and yet dangerous for presentation. Investors invest in teams, not slide decks. Don't let the slide do the talking. Investors invest in you.

Slide Formatting

We've covered the basic slide types, let's look at formatting. For example, what titles do you use, how do you organize the layout, what font and slide styles are best?

When you craft slide titles, communicate the message. If you state the message in the title, the message cannot be clearer. Many entrepreneurs use common titles like problem, product, or market. These titles communicate the topic but not the message. Notice the slide below.

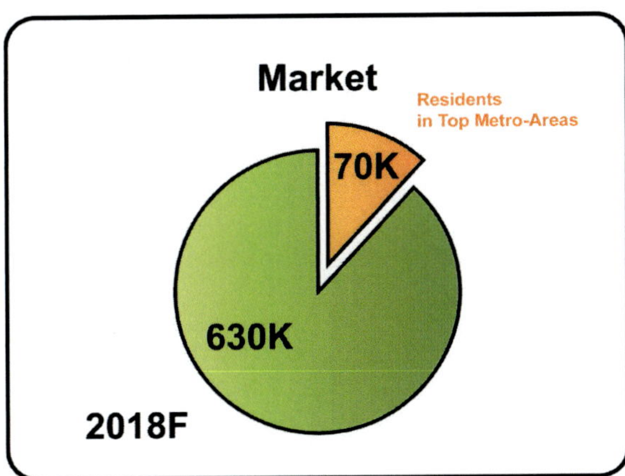

Instead of stating the topic, state the message. Notice below how a slight change to the title conveys meaning.

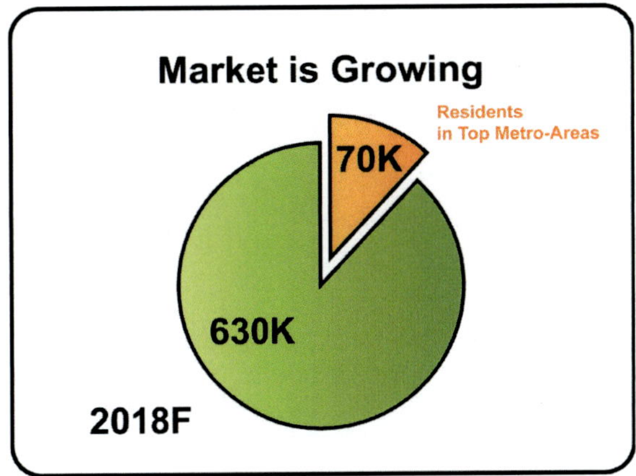

When you design slide titles, convey the message in one line using as few words as possible. Model your words the way newspapers write headlines: use only important nouns and active verbs. Here's a headline I read in today's New York Times: "Countries seek entrepreneurs from Silicon Valley." Clean, crisp, clear. Contrast this against the full sentence approach: "Many countries are seeking entrepreneurs from Silicon Valley in California." The meaning is the same, but the headline is shorter and easier to understand. Don't use full sentences for your title, make them headlines.

Let's look at another design technique. What's wrong with the slide below?

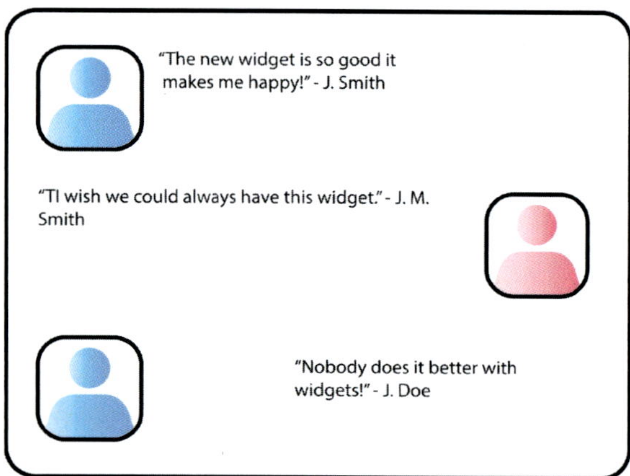

The main issue is symmetry. Asymmetrical slides cause confusion and are more difficult to absorb. Organize your slide content with symmetry. See how much more easily the slide reads when you make its contents symmetrical.

The next slide shows a list of benefits. It could be better. What do you think is wrong?

Benefits

- Extends plant life
- Easy to use
- Saves time
- Saves water

The issue is again symmetry. Notice all the benefits are squished up at the top. Balance the content within the slide area so it becomes cleaner and more symmetrical.

Benefits

- Extends plant life
- Easy to use
- Saves time
- Saves water

Many entrepreneurs also fill up space on their slides with unnecessary words or images like the slide below.

Product

- Install the product with one click through the home screen
- Cross-platform compatibility is the wave of the future
- Product lasts for 15 years at normal usage

Resist the urge. Notice how the random image distracts from the core content and creates confusion. Why add the clutter? If the image were instead removed, the focus flows to the content. This is also one reason not to place your logo on every slide in your deck.

Empty space is one of the most important elements of clean slide design. Space is luxury. People purchase huge houses full of space. Department stores display their most elegant products surrounded by space. Recently the Palo Alto Apple store here in Silicon Valley moved to a new and more impressive location full of space. ADD VALUE TO YOUR SLIDES BY NOT FILLING UP THE SPACE.

Now let's redesign this slide. First, we remove the image. Next, we clarify the technical features by converting them to easily-relatable benefits. Now we edit the slide title to convey the message. Finally, we lay out the points symmetrically. Voila!

Many Benefits

- Save time installing
- Use anywhere
- Never need to replace

Let's explore fonts, colors, and slide background. The best rule of thumb for font size is to reference Kawasaki's 10-20-30 rule: 10 slides in 20 minutes with 30-point font. 30-POINT FONT MINIMUM IS THE WAY TO GO. This makes it easy for your audience to read and deters you from adding too much text.

When it comes to colors, contrast is the way to go. To make your content easy to see, use high contrast colors between the font, images, and slide background. DARK COLORS WORK ON LIGHT BACKGROUNDS AND LIGHT COLORS WORK ON DARK BACKGROUNDS. For example, if your slides are white, use a black font. If your slides are black, use a white font. Use contrast so the content pops out of the background.

As you choose your colors, also consider what those colors represent. For example, red generally signals bad and green signals good. If you're displaying your revenue, use green for rising revenue.

When stylizing your slides, keep things simple. Avoid slide backgrounds that contain wavy lines or distract from the content. And when it comes to style, be consistent. Maintain a consistent background and consistent font. Keep it clear. Keep it simple.

Avoid animation. Animation often creates movement, and movement distracts the audience.

Finally, triple-check your slides to confirm they are error-free. If you have misspellings or other mistakes in your slide, you not only communicate low quality and poor communication, you also send the implicit signal that you don't care enough about investors to prepare thoroughly.

SECTION SUMMARY

Image Slides - Photos

- Use photos to strengthen the emotional content of your stories
- Display only one photo per slide
- Avoid adding words that distract from the photo

Image Slides - Icons

- Use icons to convey ideas so your audience can follow along
- Display no more than 4 icons at a time
- Create diagrams of icons to illustrate processes and relationships between ideas

Number slides

- Use number slides to display data
- Ensure you have a clear message, formatted data, and one chart per slide

Word slides

- Use word slides to display quotes and list benefits
- Minimize total words on slides so investors don't have to do mental work
- Keep bulleted points to only a few words and never wrap to a second line
- Avoid slides that speak for the presenter

Formatting

- Use slide titles to state slide messages
- Organize your slides so they have symmetry
- Avoid filling white space with excessive info or unnecessary distractions
- Use fonts, colors, and backgrounds that keep your slides clear and consistent

EXERCISE: DESIGN YOUR SLIDES

1. Review the messages you identified in the previous exercise set. Create a slide for each message. Title each slide with the message in headline form.

2. Create a benefits slide to support your solution. Next, create a numbers slide that shows your market size.

3. Create and organize your team slide to emphasize details that matter. Remove all other background. If you're not sure whether to keep something on the slide, remove it. Any hesitation suggests it's not the most important info on the slide.

4. Review the slides you just designed and confirm the following:

- The slides are symmetrical
- The minimum font size of all text is 30-point
- All text and images use colors that contrast with their background

Congrats on designing great slides! You can use these design techniques to create slides for all the messages you identified in the previous slide deck exercise.

More on Slides

Balance

There are three primary types of slides: image slides, number slides, and word slides. All of them have their uses. Image slides with photos are effective at conveying emotion (story). Image slides using icons are effective at clarifying complexity (credibility). Number slides are a solid way to display facts and figures (data). Word slides work for listing benefits (audience value). Each slide type has its function. To decide what slide type to use, first identify the message you want to convey.

TO REDUCE THE EFFORT ON INVESTORS, LEAN MORE TOWARDS IMAGES. WHILE A HEALTHY SLIDE DECK WILL CONTAIN A MIX OF DIFFERENT SLIDE TYPES, RECALL THAT IMAGES ARE THE EASIEST TO PROCESS MENTALLY, WHILE WORD SLIDES TAKE THE MOST MENTAL WORK.

First and Last Slides

How do the rules of slide design apply to the first and last slides? Here's a quick discourse: Many companies like Apple simply use their company logo to represent the first slide. Simplicity. You can also add a line of text such as: "Prepared for Investor on mm/dd/yy."

The first slide starts the presentation, but your last slide might very well be the most influential slide in your deck. After you finish your pitch, you spend the rest of the time talking with investors and answering questions. During this time, your last slide hangs unobtrusively on the screen. It stays up the longest. You could waste the slide by showing words like "the end," or even worse, a question mark.

Better to use the last slide to your advantage. Display audience value on the last slide. You could list benefits that show your product is the best in the business; you could display your current customers; you could even show your revenue. Use your last slide to support your case for investment.

Email Slide Deck

Oftentimes investors will ask you to email a slide deck prior to meeting. The deck needs to speak for itself because you're not there. Simple slides don't work in email, so you can't use your live deck; you need a second deck to send to investors. What should this deck look like? When I interviewed one investment firm, they said partners typically use the email deck to gauge the idea and run the numbers.

To build an effective email deck, follow the 4-Point Pitch formula and focus on Elements of Influence. A good email deck flows logically, and the 4-Point formula gives you that flow. Likewise, prove your points by adding elements that emphasize credibility, audience value, data and story.

When you design your email deck, make it info-rich. For example, write out the problem and the problem pains. Expand on solution features and benefits. Show more numbers. Highlight key phrases in your slides to draw investor attention. As you design your slides, keep them easy to read. Investors have limited time, and it's unlikely they're going to sit down to read an essay. Remember, concision is more important than content!

You're probably already very good at designing detailed slides. This is the tradition of the business world. Detailed decks kill live presentations, but they work just fine for email.

SECTION SUMMARY

- Recall that image slides are easiest for investors to process
- Make your first slide simple by displaying your logo
- Design your last slide to show investment value
- Craft an info-rich email deck that follows the 4-Point flow

EXERCISE: EDIT YOUR EMAIL DECK

1. Create an outline for your email deck based on the 4-Point Pitch formula.

2. When you begin organizing slides for your email deck, title each slide with a clear message and add text in the slide to explain the details. Be sure to emphasize the messages you identified in the previous slide exercises.

An email deck is often the key that leads to live meetings. By following the 4-Point formula, you make your deck interesting and more likely to open meeting-room doors.

Conclusion

Investors invest in you. General Catalyst Partners principal, Niko Bonatsos, once mentioned that his firm has invested in several very early stage startups that pitched without slides. Remember the pitch starts with you. When it comes to slides, use your slide deck to enhance your words. Simple slides reinforce your pitch and ensure persuasive power. Keep slides simple by showing only one message per slide.

THE LESS INFORMATION YOU FIT INTO YOUR SLIDES, THE MORE POWERFUL THEY APPEAR. LESS IS MORE.

CHAPTER 6

FORWARD TO FUNDING

6. FORWARD TO FUNDING

Chapter 6 Forward to Funding

Companies that win funding, winners like GetAround and Mint.com, use a pitch that is part science and part art. Their success depends not just on the content of their pitch but on the skills used to deliver that content. In the negotiation book *Getting More,* Professor Stuart Diamond of Wharton says that 90 percent of negotiation success comes from the people involved and the process used, while only 10 percent comes from substance, facts, and figures. Assume these same stats apply to your pitch.

When you follow the 3 basic principles, you focus on the people involved. For investors, the purpose of a pitch is to identify investment value: low risk high return. To ensure they hear this message, concision is more important than content. Remember also that investors invest in you. You are the key to a successful startup, not your data nor your slides. Your clarity and logic impact how investors evaluate you.

By organizing your content into a 4-Point Pitch, you follow a process that makes it easy for investors to understand your main message. Effective pitches almost always start with a problem, move to a solution, then to the market and finally the business. The most important points are supported with a unique blend of influential elements including credibility, audience value, data, and story. Make it clear, make it interesting, make it real, and make it meaningful.

If you capture and hold investor attention, your words gain traction in investors' minds. Grab attention by starting your pitch with benefits, intriguing info, or investor involvement. Hold attention using current events, enthusiasm, and contrast. As you dialogue, ask questions and adjust your pitch to achieve even greater connection. Through this process, utilize simple slides to reinforce your key messages without drawing attention away from you. Less is more.

You'll also begin to notice a significant increase in your self-confidence. Knowing how to dialogue and practicing your pitch removes fear of the unknown and gives you guidance during investor encounters. This self-confidence reflects investment-worthiness.

Pitching is a science and an art, and now you know the science and have artistic guidelines. The next time you attend a pitch event and watch others, the fun starts. You'll see pitches from a whole new perspective. When you watch others, you'll recognize how failure to follow the 4-Point Pitch Formula loses the audience, as was the case with the startup Lumier (discussed in Chapter 2). You'll admire the influential elements used by entrepreneurs to support their points as shown by Kindara (discussed in Chapter 3).

And when you stand up to deliver your own pitch, you will stand out with clarity. Since many of these techniques derive from research on effective persuasion, marketing, and business communications, these skills can be applied universally. While writing this book, I've met with colleagues to propose new ideas and new business plans. In every case, I used the principles and formula in this book to move my case forward.

In time, you'll discover that the skills here extend beyond fundraising to win buy-in from other spheres. You'll win more customers by aligning with their problems and presenting benefits. You'll manage your team more effectively through presenting a clear vision and strategy. You'll even be able to attract media attention when you tie your startup to current events and highlight values that others care about.

FUNDRAISING IS A BRUTAL PROCESS. IT'S ONE OF THE TOP CHALLENGES YOU FACE WHEN BUILDING A SOLID COMPANY, AND ONE OF THE REASONS MANY STARTUPS FAIL. BUT WINNING INVESTMENT IS ONE OF THE GREATEST TRIUMPHS. YOU'VE TAKEN SERIOUS STEPS TO IMPROVE YOUR PITCH SKILLS BY READING THIS BOOK. NOW USE THESE SKILLS TO GO OUT THERE AND WIN FUNDING!

Acknowledgements

Success is 10% inspiration, 90% perspiration. And 900% support. Nowhere was this more obvious than the creation of this book. First and foremost I thank JD Schramm, who supported the birth of this project as well as a nascent craft. He is an inspiration for the generosity of the human spirit.

I am grateful to the cherished memory of my grandparents Estelle and Joseph Lipp, whose munificent gift supported this endeavor. The fruits of their perspiration gave me health and warm hearth as I toiled with words. And their love, which is the source of everything.

Baking a book requires learning from the best. I am fortunate to have worked with Jerry Weissman and David Woodward, receiving continual tips on presentation and teaching techniques. There is a quote I attribute to Eckhart Tolle which, if memory serves me right, is this: we all have fire in us. But by being close to those masters who have already found their fire, we begin to blaze brighter.

My appreciation also goes to Sonia Oster, who is responsible for all things visual. As an expert in verbal communications, I frequently quote research showing that effective presentation is 55% visual, a statistic which I promptly forgot when writing. Sonia's admonishment, and ultimately the beautiful graphics she created, reminded me of the evident.

Many people contributed to the quality of this book so that it shined accurately and artistically. I thank in particular Steve Ciesinski, Ivory Madison, and Diana Roome. I plundered Steve's knowledge to the limits, unabashedly, with joy. Ivory gave advice that made this book a more complete resource and cautioned me in many extremely useful respects. Diana my editor taught me rules of English language that I hadn't known existed.

Special thanks go to Meta Mehling and Gayle Laakmann McDowell for knowledge that led me on my path. A book is a special kind of product that takes guidance to create. Meta changed my perspective and helped elicit the idea, while Gayle introduced the tools and techniques to bring the idea to fruition.

Thanks to Kenzi Wang and Alexi Nedelchev, who model the entrepreneurial spirit and tenacity to succeed. They wrangled me from Stanford to work in the startup world. We laughed, we cried, we had a lot of fun. Ultimately, we grew.

I also thank the many proofreaders of this book, including in particular Eleni Lialiamou who gave deeper insight into markets. And like most entrepreneurs, I needed and welcomed the positive feedback to keep me motivated.

Finally, behind every book is an author, and behind every author are people who kindle the author's spirit. To my many friends unmentioned here. I love you all.

Resources

Pitches worth watching:

Badgeville	http://www.youtube.com/watch?v=UZGhGtF2xeA
Enigma	http://tinyurl.com/d238b5l
GetAround	http://tinyurl.com/3gduxf9
Kindara	http://vimeo.com/46512342
LifeSaver	http://tinyurl.com/nuntco
Loopt	http://www.youtube.com/watch?v=Khhld_WG7RA
RidePal	http://www.youtube.com/watch?v=PxElr5ltL0M
Stormpulse	http://tinyurl.com/mraaq5o

More advice from:

Paul Graham	http://www.paulgraham.com/fundraising.html
Reid Hoffman	http://reidhoffman.org/linkedin-pitch-to-greylock/ (on Series B)
Guy Kawasaki	http://tinyurl.com/l9uqkhy
David Rose	http://www.ted.com/talks/david_s_rose_on_pitching_to_vcs.html
Robert Scoble	http://drt.fm/robert-scoble/
Peter Thiel	http://tinyurl.com/knnvh46

Index

Made in the USA
Middletown, DE
03 October 2023